Leon Mandrake

THE REAL MANDRAKE THE MAGICIAN

LINDA AND LON MANDRAKE

FriesenPress

Suite 300 - 990 Fort St
Victoria, BC, V8V 3K2
Canada

www.friesenpress.com

ISBN
978-1-5255-3470-6 (Hardcover)
978-1-5255-3471-3 (Paperback)
978-1-5255-3472-0 (eBook)

1. BIOGRAPHY & AUTOBIOGRAPHY, ENTERTAINMENT & PERFORMING ARTS

Distributed to the trade by The Ingram Book Company

TABLE OF CONTENTS

I dedicate The Real Mandrake the Magician to my loving parents,
Eric and Kay Redden, who always encouraged me in my creative writing.

ACKNOWLEDGEMENT

Thanks to the Mandrake family for their encouragement in the creation of this book, *The Real Mandrake the Magician.* And I am indebted to my writers' club, the Pen and Inklings, for their great critiques and advice. At the core of it all are the wonderful memories and stories of Velvet and Lon. Thank you, Lon, for scanning what seemed like a thousand photos. And Katrina, our daughter, I give you a big hug for holding my hand through the jungle of computer formatting. It was truly a family effort: Mandrake's wife, son, daughter-in-law, and granddaughter – I know he would be pleased.

INTRODUCTION

How I Met the Mandrakes

A little background about the author: I was born Linda Caroline Redden in the picturesque seaside town of Chester, Nova Scotia. It is home to North America's largest keel-boat race week with a history of 163 years of racing. Except for the race week in August, it is a quiet little town that afforded me a great childhood. In many ways it is similar to the fictional town of Maycomb in *To Kill a Mockingbird* by Harper Lee (without the racial troubles), and my father was nearly a double for the gentle and noble character, Atticus Finch. We all walked to school in those days and had the run of the town; we knew everyone. My best friend, Patsy Derek, eventually moved all the way to Victoria, British Columbia with her family (her father was in the navy). We kept up a correspondence and at about the age of twenty we cooked up the idea of renting an apartment in Vancouver for the summer of 1968. How were we to support ourselves? She had worked as a secretary in Victoria and I, in my third year of university at Mount Allison in New Brunswick, had taken some secretarial courses along with my regular Bachelor of Arts degree courses. We would be typists. So I flew out to Vancouver and we settled in, surviving on amazingly small money by today's standards. We had a wonderful summer together. I remember my first and lasting impression of Vancouver was the sight of those amazing mountains at the end of Granville Street as I stood by the Hudson's Bay store.

One day I grabbed a bus and explored the University of British Columbia. I decided I wanted to stay in Vancouver if I could transfer my courses out west, so I applied. UBC held Mount Allison in high regard and my marks were good, so they gave me credit for everything I had taken before (something rather rare I heard).

I enrolled in September. My parents sent my winter wardrobe out in a huge trunk and worried, I know, to have their only child so far from home. I studied hard not to waste their money and to make them proud of me. UBC did not like to grant you a degree if you were only with them one year, so instead of just finishing my last year of a Bachelor of Arts program, they had me switch to the five-year program of Bachelor of Education, giving me two years on their campus. To my surprise I was destined to be a teacher. The enroller thought I needed extra courses to complete the switch, and so I ended up with seven courses instead of the regular full-year five.

When I began the second year, a different enroller was shocked I'd had such an unnecessarily heavy load and wondered how I had coped. I remembered my exhaustion and terrible eyestrain from all the reading and essay writing and just smiled. The final year with teaching practicums seemed easier.

It was in the university dining room of Totem Park residence that I met my husband-to-be, Lon (Lonny) Mandrake. He phoned me for a coffee date as soon as I returned to my room in residence. I recognized that he was the darkly handsome fellow studying microbiology and genetics, who'd been sitting at our table. We hit it off well and were soon dating steadily. When he said his father was Mandrake the Magician, I didn't know what to think. I'd had little experience with magic growing up.

Soon he drove me home to meet his parents and to stay for Velvet's wonderful roast-pork dinner. I was understandably nervous.

My first impression of the Mandrakes was a lasting one. As we walked into the long living room, Leon, the magician, entered from the right and Velvet, his assistant and wife of many years, entered from the left. They came together as a couple to shake my hand and welcome me with easy chatter and warm friendliness. Although it had seemed like a stage entrance to me at the time, I realize now Leon had come from his office where he'd been working, and Velvet had been in the bathroom on the left, running a little late in preparation for our visit no doubt. I learned later that Mandrake's mother (he said she was a kind, honest, and hardworking woman) had come from Nova Scotia too, and when they heard I was Nova Scotian, they suspected I might be a keeper.

Three years later, we married with receptions in Vancouver and Nova Scotia. The years rolled by, both of us teaching high school – Lon in science, and myself as an English teacher. I occasionally saw the Mandrakes perform if they were working locally. I knew them as kind and friendly parents. They welcomed me with open arms and babysat a lot as our family grew. When they toured the east of Canada, my parents were delighted to entertain them and have them stay over.

Lon and I lived in the New Westminster family home for fifteen years before we bought our own house. Lon began managing his dad, booking many university tours in the seventies and eighties. We were trained in mentalism by Mandrake. He seemed pleased when we developed our own show and started performing. When I mentioned nervousness, Mandrake said, "It's that nervous energy that gives you the edge to be good; even seasoned performers feel it." One day he asked me if I had ever considered doing illusions and had me step into one of the larger ones. It turned out that I was too tall since it had been built for tiny Velvet, and I was truthfully a little relieved but flattered to have been asked to try out. When we returned from a mentalist performance, all naturally high from the excitement and challenge of it, I saw the twinkle in Mandrake's eye as he seemed pleased we liked to perform. The magic bug that had bitten him had begun to nibble on us too.

Why I Wrote The Real Mandrake the Magician

Foremost, I wanted the world to know the genius and charm of Mandrake. He was a fantastic magician and deserves to be remembered. Secondly, I wanted all those wonderful family stories and pictures to last more than one generation, for my grandchildren's grandchildren to know their famous Mandrake relatives. And finally, because other books on Mandrake have been chronologically correct but have failed in capturing his unique personality, I wanted people to know the real Mandrake the Magician.

PREFACE

"Look at this! There's a secret compartment in the bottom of this trunk."

My husband stepped carefully through the Mandrake show suitcases and wooden crates to find me holding open the lid of a gargantuan trunk.

"See, it looks like a drawer from above but the bottom is hollow – listen," and I tapped.

"Oh, I remember this one. Push in, the wall is spring-loaded; it'll open."

And it did. A purple velvet cloth was concealing something large. I pulled and out rolled a grapefruit-sized ball – a glass ball, a huge, clear marble.

"Hey, I wondered where that was; it's Dad's crystal ball – careful," he added as I lifted it up.

"It's really heavy."

"Here, put it in its holder," Lon said as he reached in the enclosure to find the support for the globe; a silver circle supported by a tripod of three dragons.

We pushed the garage mess back against the wall and made room for the stand and crystal on the work bench.

"It's beautiful."

"And very old. You can still buy glass balls from magic dealers, but this is a perfect real crystal, made in Germany I think. Look inside, no imperfections. Some cheap ones have tiny bubbles or specks."

"Think how many people have looked into this with questions or troubles. Think what stories it could tell," I said.

"And it was Alexander's crystal originally. He was a magician and mentalist in the 1910s and '20s – very popular in his day. When Dad's own career was building, he went to Los Angeles to visit him. Dad told me that a tall, lean man peeked out the door to say that the great Alexander couldn't be disturbed. But Dad persisted, since he was a great admirer of Alexander's. He said, 'Tell him I'm Leon Mandrake and I've come a long way to see him. Tell him it was because of all the Alexander posters all over my hometown of New Westminster, Canada, and because of his newspaper columns giving readers advice that I got into this crazy business.' Alexander had probably heard of the up and coming Mandrake, and was flattered, so Dad was invited in. He said the lanky fellow led him into an inner room. There was a stage prop throne against the far wall. Instead of leaving to call Alexander, he suddenly stepped up and sat down on the throne himself, saying, 'You wanted to see me?' he asked."

"A throne? Seriously?" I asked.

"He was quite a character – suspected of being a rum runner in secret as well as incredibly rich from his mystic, see-into-the-future shows. Dad and he got along famously; they talked magic for hours."

"What kind of questions did he answer?"

"Where did Grandpa hide the gold? Where's my lost wedding ring? He had a huge following in the 1920s. He even wrote a series of books entitled *The Real Inner Secrets of Psychology*. He always said psychology would one day be taught in the schools as a real science (to the ridicule of his peers). I wonder where that book is?" and Lon started looking in cardboard boxes as he talked. "Dad left with several magic props, the crystal ball, and some ideas for the show. Years later, two years before Alexander died, he said he wanted to leave his magic to a worthy magician, so he sold Dad the rights to the Alexander name, his publicity materials, several illusions, and quite a few costumes."

"Rights to his name?"

"Yeah, didn't you know Dad performed for a while as Alexander, as well as doing his own show? You remember that promo photo of Dad in Alexander's turban gazing into the crystal."

"Oh, it was in the hall for a while," I remembered, which was lucky since we had so the many framed show posters all over our walls. Too many I felt, but Lon loved putting them up and changing them around. There was even

a signed one of Siegfried and Roy (from well before the tiger attacked Roy) in our bathroom.

I gazed into the crystal. The cluttered garage with no fewer than twenty-seven (I had counted) white metal suitcases with Mandrake stenciled on their sides was reflected in a circular shape. But as you tilted your head slightly, the view changed and gave the impression you were being drawn in.

"Found it." Lon held up Alexander's black, hardcover handbook and then started to laugh. It's subtitled, *1924, Volume III – The Psychology of Sex*. Hey," he teased, "I've got to read this!"

But I wasn't listening. "If only the ball could speak," I murmured. "Can you reveal the past as well as the future?" I asked it. Looking deep into the center of the glass, I found it difficult to look away, as if the crystal were holding me.

Leo and Velvet Mandrake performing as Alexander in the TV show, The Great Alexander Show, 1955

Alexander, the "Man who Knows", sitting on his throne

Leon Mandrake as Alexander on his The Great Alexander TV show, 1955

Leon (Lon) Mandrake Jr. , mentalist, 1990's

THE MAGNIFICENCE OF MANDRAKE

(magnificent: adj. splendid in appearance and excellent in quality)

Leon Mandrake and his lovely assistants performed in many prestigious venues over the years, including the Orpheum Theatre in Los Angeles, the Civic Opera House in Chicago, the Lyric Theatre in Minneapolis, the Civic Opera Auditorium in St. Paul, Minnesota, an eleven-week hold over at the President Hotel, Kansas City, a record-breaking run at Detroit's Bowery, many engagements in Reno and Las Vegas, and the Kaiser Dome in Hawaii. At the height of his career he toured for MCA with two buses and seventeen assistants.

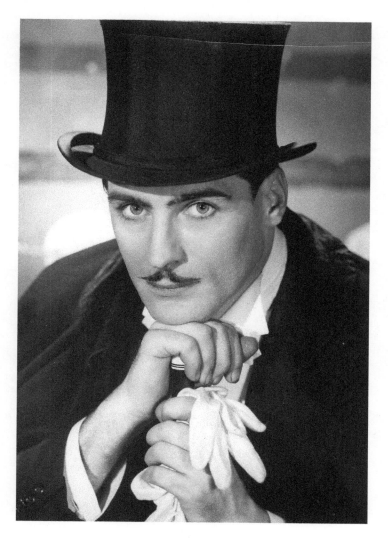

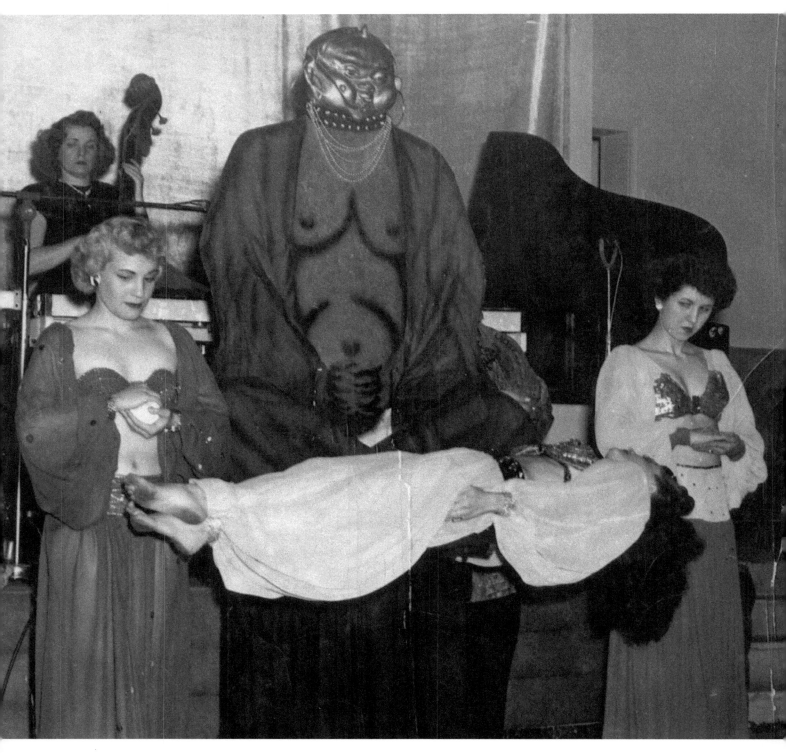

As times changed, Mandrake was one of the few who was able to adapt a stage show to nightclubs. He was the first to float a woman in mid-air completely surrounded by an audience. (no curtains or props to hide any magical gimmicks).

Mandrake was the first to use the larger balloons
to make novelty animals for the show.

Mandrake was the first to combine a steel substitution trunk with a quick costume change.
And not only had his black suit tuned white but he was casually smoking a lit cigarette (how times change)
as he emerged from the tied and locked trunk where Velvet had been confined 3 seconds before.
Magicians couldn't see how he was so fast unless he had a twin...wrong!

His signature piece was his dancing handkerchief in a bottle called Katy King after the famous spiritualist who knew Sir Arthur Conan Doyle, author of Sherlock Holmes. A knotted cloth was put into a jug and corked shut. With a wave of Mandrake's hand it came to life, responded to his voice, popped the cork and danced on the table; a metal ring showed there were no controlling wires. He coaxed her back into the jug and corked her in again.

PROGRAM

PART I

MANDRAKE:
>   Gloves to Doves
>   Floating in Mid-Air
>   Enchanting Cane
>   Silks from Nowhere
>   Flower from Flames
>   Meet Peter Rabbit - - Proverbial Magicial Assistant

TRANSPOSITION OF A BOTTLE, ORANGE, AND BRAN
>   Amazing, simply amazing . . . .

JUST A BIT OF FUN WITH SOME GOLF BALLS
>   A bit of Manipulation Direct from the 19th Hole

BIRDS FROM ANOTHER DIMENSION
>   Proving the Impossible is Possible

FLIGHT OF THE RABBITS
>   An Impossible Trip

A DECK OF CARDS AND A LITTLE SOFT MUSIC
>   A Tribute to the Late Howard Thurston

SHOOTING THRU A WOMAN
>   Execution of Mati Hari - - Is it Legal to Commit Murder

A LESSON IN MAGIC
>   Wherein the Young Generation becomes Magicians

RIBBONSATION
>   Mutilation, Confiscation, Restoration

THE TEMPLE OF MOGAR
>   From the Purple Hills of Hindustan comcs a Strange and
>   Weird Tale . . . . .

BEHOLD A MIRACLE!
>   And the Tale of Mogar Ends

POP-AWAY
>   Have one on Me

EXPERIMENTS IN EXTRA SENSORY PERCEPTION
>   A Mental Problem

SLAVE GIRLS OF THEBES
>   Centuries Ago in the Land of the Pyramids, along the
>   Banks of the Nile River. . . . . . .

PLEXIGLASS CASE
>   The Modern Touch

MANDRAKES SENSATIONAL ESCAPE FROM A
WELDED STEEL BARREL
>   Mandrake will attempt to escape from a welded steel
>   barrel in 90 seconds You are invited to bring your own
>   locks and handcuffs.. Inspect the barrel in the lobby.

PART 11

A SUCCESSION OF SURPRISES
>   The Closer you Watch--The Closer You Watch

THE DREAM OF KING MIDAS
>   A Magician's answer to Inflation.

PARASOLA
>   Anything Can happen

AN ORIENTNL PUZZLE
>   The Chinese Bowls of Plenty

A MAGICAL LESSON
>   Egg Foo Yung a la Mandrake

FLOWERS FOR MADAM
>   Especially for the Ladies

KATY KINGS CONTROL
>   An Adventure With an "Ordinary" deck af Cards and
>   a Friendly Spook

THE MYSTERY OF THF RED CHEST
>   In again Out Again

DOVES AND MORE DOVES
>   Is the Supply Unlimited?

ENCHANTED PAGODA
>   A Trip Into Chinese Mythology

CHINESE STEEL BANDS
>   A magician's classic originated by Chinese jugglers in
>   2000 B.C. If you've seen it before, you'll enjoy it again
>   ---if you haven't seen it before, you have a treat in store.

SMOKE GETS IN YOUR EYES
>   May I borrow a Cigarette, please?

HYPNOTISM
>   A Demonstration of the "Eeil Eye"--Voodoo or Science?

MANDRAKE'S FAMOUS BLACK IS WHITE ILLUSION
>   So amazing you won't believe it even after you see it---
>   but you will remember it all your life.

PROGRAM SUBJECT TO CHANGE WITHOUT NOTICE

Mandrake was unique because of the fast pace of his show. Famous magician, Zany Blaney, said, "Mandrake does more magic in his first ten minutes than most magicians do in a whole show".

Mandrake had girls in bunny costumes long before Playboy Hugh Hefner did the same.

Mandrake's Guillotine illusion and talking decapitated head: test the blade by splitting a cabbage in half, then lop off your assistant's head and place it on a sword on an armchair. The eyes open and the head speaks with Mandrake. Suddenly he throws the head into the audience; they catch a cabbage.

Mandrake's Pagoda illusion: The assistant hides in the tiny doll house and closes the roof doors. Leon thrusts many swords into the house. The audience sees a criss-cross of blades when the house is opened but no assistant. Then Mandrake closes up the roof, spins the pagoda once about and she emerges unharmed.

Mandrake's version of shooting a lady was a favorite. He shot the rifle at Velvet, the bullet piercing a selected card placed on her stomach and then lodging in a target six feet behind her. A ribbon attached to the bullet had trailed through her body as she recovered and walked toward Mandrake.

THE REAL MANDRAKE THE MAGICIAN

Mandrake's Lady in a Fishbowl (Jug) was truly amazing. How did Velvet shrink to the size of Tinkerbell of Peter Pan fame and then live happily inside a glass jug?

Mandrake's card house illusion began with a pile of playing cards that grew magically into a tiny house. The big surprise was Velvet was hiding inside it.

THE REAL MANDRAKE THE MAGICIAN

Mandrake's Transposition illusion had two beautiful girls appear then disappear and then reappear again in a glass box.

THE REAL MANDRAKE THE MAGICIAN

Mandrake did three versions of sawing a lady in half: buzz saw, cross-cut saw, and sawing a lady in half with a ribbon. Pictured is the buzz saw at the Stadium show at the Pacific National Exhibition, Vancouver, B. C. in 1964.

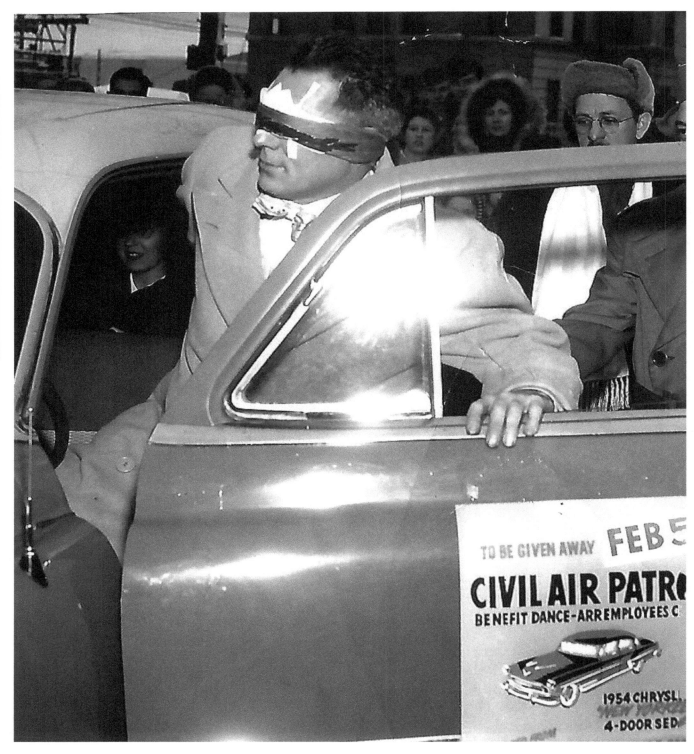

Alaska

THE REAL MANDRAKE THE MAGICIAN

Mandrake would promote his upcoming shows with a blindfold drive through town.

*Mandrake produced trained doves and fan-tailed pigeons that flew out over the audience
and then landed faithfully on his lovely assistant.*

THE REAL MANDRAKE THE MAGICIAN

Versatile Mandrake did everything: dancing as a young man (he called himself "a Hoofer"), a vent act, sleight of hand, card manipulations, fire-eating, large illusions, fortune telling, hypnotism, mentalism, and escapes.

Mandrake escaped from nailed boxes ,sealed steel barrels and large city jails to promote his upcoming shows.

Velvet became Carlotta, the headless woman, with the assistance of George Patey (left) and Bill Eliason (right). The illusion was presented as a scientific experiment to see if the human body could survive without a head. The set was quite elaborate and authentic looking and was even covered by local television. Velvet remembers the long stint where she could only hear the audience reactions. Two older women were saying to each other, "Oh poor thing! Why don't they just let her die?"

Favorites on Mandrake's shows were the floating table and tube productions of an amazing number of items like water-filled fish bowls as seen above.

Mandrake, as a show promotion, would hypnotize volunteer celebrities to be seen in a store mindlessly doing something like riding a bike through the aisles.

Many people were mesmerized by Mandrake's hypnotic green eyes.

Mandrake created a Doorway to Nowhere where a door in a frame would be fully exposed for inspection; its door would be closed and then opened again to reveal Leon and Velvet making their grand entrance from nowhere.

Mandrake, performing at the Pacific National Exhibition in Vancouver, B. C. for ten years running, developed a Magic of Light show. Inside a television a skull turned into a living head of an Egyptian princess. And he produced lit electric light bulbs from mid air in 1958.

THE REAL MANDRAKE THE MAGICIAN

Mandrake was presented with the prestigious Performing Fellowship for a lifetime in magic at the Magic Castle in Hollywood in 1978.(See page 113 for details)

Mandrake had several TV shows (2 weekly Alexander the Great shows) in the 1950's, guest spots on children's shows, a 1963 special, The Manipulators in 1970, a CBC Hallowe'en special in 1972, a Beach Combers episode in 1977, and various interviews including Fifth Estate. Mary Ungerleider's 45 minute film, Mandrake, a Magical Life, came out in 2001; the haunting history of an unforgettable man and his eternal magic.

THE REAL MANDRAKE THE MAGICIAN

Mandrake had a very successful lecture circuit in over fifty universities and colleges in Canada and the U.S.A., speaking on topics like these at Simon Fraser University, Vancouver, B.C. in 1971:

- Sept. 26: Gambling and Trickery
- Oct. 3: Ancient and Modern Magic
- Oct. 10: Mind Mystics
- Oct. 17: Séances and Spiritualism
- Oct. 24: Fortune Tellers, Mind Readers, and Psychics
- Nov. 7: Illegal Confidence Games (demos of "short change" etc.)
- Nov. 14: Legal Confidence Games (incl. pyramid selling)

EARLY DAYS

Mandrake (Leon John Arthur Giglio) was born April 11, 1911 at Oak Harbor, Whidbey Island, Washington, U.S.A. to Arthur and Harriet Giglio. His parents had met when Arthur was working in New Westminster, B.C. as a professional chef. They married and with Carl, Harriet's four-year-old son by a previous marriage, moved to Arthur's hundred-acre farm on Orcas Island, Washington, on the west coast. (Arthur's younger brother was Beniamino Gigli, the operatic tenor of international fame.) Unfortunately, the marriage ended in divorce in just a few years, and Harriet, with her two sons, moved back to Canada to live with her mother and sister, Mildred, in New Westminster.

To a large degree, by working in the post office, Mildred was supporting the family; her mother, grandmother, and two brothers, John and Bert. Bert had been disabled after falling from a tree at age thirteen and was a bed-ridden invalid until he died at age sixty-six. Mildred had developed a unique filing system that made postal sorting much faster. In that chauvinistic era, her male boss took most of the credit for her idea and Mildred was left with thanks and a small raise in pay. (She worked there thirty-five years.) Nevertheless, she welcomed her sister Harriet and her two boys into the home until they could find a place of their own.

When Leon enrolled in the elementary school, the teacher mispronounced his Italian last name, calling him "gig lee oh" instead of "gee lee oh" and thereafter Leon was nicknamed "Gig" by his predominantly English classmates. As he grew older, he sometimes used just Leon for shows or his brother's last name, Jackson, in self- defense. In later life, when he was asked whether Mandrake was his birth name, he often looked uncomfortable and side-stepped the question, which made the issue seem unduly mysterious. An interviewer at Los Angeles' Magic Castle once put him on the spot about his birth name after having been specifically

asked not to mention that issue. The interview was being taped. Leon graciously explained that entertainers often take stage names and implied that a rose is a rose by any other name and what is all the fuss about anyway? But the truth was that his early experience of prejudicial treatment because of his foreign last name had stayed with him all his life. In the early 1940s he had his name legally changed to Mandrake.

Auntie Mildred gave Leon a magic set as an eighth-birthday present and his interest in magic grew from that moment. He read every book on the subject at the city library. (He remained an avid reader all his life.) And he also practiced with a local candy merchant who dabbled in sleight of hand. At the age of eleven, Leon performed at the Edison theatre on Columbia Street in New Westminster, calling himself "The Wiz" after the magician in *The Wizard of Oz*. (He had read the whole series of *Oz* books.) He was on call at the theatre for any performers that didn't show. Looking back on those days, Leon said he was so nervous when he performed, that his knees knocked together.

As a divorced single mother, Harriet found supporting two children difficult in those days of scant work for women and inequality of pay. At the end of grade six, Leon left school to work in a shingle mill to help with the family finances. In the summer, Harriet would take the boys camping in White Rock, augmenting the food budget with fresh fish, clams, and blackberries. This measure of thrift was seen by Leon as a great adventure. All his life, he had the knack of looking on the bright side of things and of improvising. Like many of his generation, he enjoyed finding a bargain and the challenge of finding a solution. He often said, "If you have a problem, look outside the box." In other words, take another look at it from a different perspective and a solution may appear. One of his hobbies, in later years, was to use older pieces of jewelry, often found in second-hand stores, in order to create new designs. And when a fire in an Alaskan nightclub destroyed all Velvet's costumes, to decorate the new outfits Leon found replacement feathers (which were otherwise impossible to find) in feather dusters at the local Salvation Army store.

At the age of fourteen, Leon was selling peanuts and popcorn at the PNE back when its location was in New Westminster at Queen's Park. Nat Bailey, an older boy who was selling beside him, grew up to be the founder of the White Spot chain of restaurants. The huge buildings for the exhibition, shown in old photos, are long gone. Leon, at fourteen, was suggested as the best in town to the owner, Ma Counts, who needed a local magician. He was hired to perform in the big tent. Part of Leon's show required a Princess Thora for at least one of the illusions (swords in the box). The young magician improvised with broomsticks for swords, and a good friend, Jackie Giles, dressed in a dress and wig as the princess. Leon would laugh, as he recalled how much fun he and "the lovely Thora" had in those days. It was beneficial that Leon was allowed to use anything left behind by previous entertainers. From his reading on magic, he recognized most of it and he set about learning how to use it.

Leon tried to see every professional magician show that came into town. He was hired

by the famous Ralph Richards Company to help out with the doves and rabbits used in the performances. He learnt a lot from Richards, who thought Leon had promise, and when the show left New Westminster, Leon, at the age of sixteen, was taken on as an assistant and

Two photos of Leon at age 16-17 with his penciled-in mustache so he would look older.

went on tour with it. When the tour finished in Winnipeg, he worked as a magician by himself, doing shows across the prairies all the way back home. Photos of Leon, at this age, show him to be a tall, sophisticated-looking young man, who could easily pass for much older than he was.

Leon then enrolled in a New Westminster school of business and later, supported by his father, in one in the States. He excelled in typing, with his exceptional manual dexterity, and easily won provincial and state speed contests. However, Leon was never employed in business, because his love of magic and performing had taken over.

Mandrake was a young man in his twenties during the Depression (the Dirty Thirties). In later years he recalled waiting nightly for the hotel room rates to lower after midnight before getting a place to sleep. In Seattle, he ran into an up and coming comedian, Bob Hope, doing the same thing. Around this time, Leon was in a serious car accident. His vehicle, with the notorious suicide doors that opened on opposite hinges to the cars of today, ran through an unmarked intersection at night and down an embankment. Leon was pinned beneath the car. So much damage was done to one leg, that the doctors feared he would either not live, or if he did survive, would never walk again.

In hospital, a priest was called in for the last rites. He asked if Leon would give the hundred-acre farm and his life insurance to the church. When Leon said he wanted to make sure his mother was looked after, the priest said, "That woman is a divorcee and deserves nothing," or words to that effect. The Catholic Church clearly did not approve of divorce. Leon grew so angry for the mother he loved, that this gave him the strength to live and fight (he explained). He spent months in hospital, exercising and wearing a leg brace. He wore it for nearly a year, until one day, he was so fed up with it that he threw it into the Fraser River

in New Westminster. With typical strength of character and determination, he exercised and built up the muscle in the front of his leg to compensate for the missing back calf muscle. For the rest of his life, he was able to walk and with only a slight limp.

Leon Mandrake's Family Tree

6 Generations

Annie MacDonald   **1**

John Wagner _____Rebecca MacDonald   **2**

William (Billy)   John   Mildred   Emily   Harriet   (Al)Bert

Alfred Jackson_____Harriet Wagner

Carl Jackson

Arthur Giglio _____ Harriet Wagner   **3**

Leon

Leon_____ Lola (Narda) Wilson

Leon _____Louise (Velvet) Salerno

Leon (Jr.) (Lon)   Ronald   Kimball (Kim)   Geelia (Jill)   **4**

Linda Redden   Cecelia Campbell   Jamie Ulrich   Lorna Boshman

Katrina   Leon(Lonny)   Eric   Sean   Jerome   Kala   Jade   **5**

Ian Coulas   Stacy Johnston   Jason Parleir   Crystal Loving   Lior Rosenthal

Shyann   Ethan   Logan   Rayne   Kalie   Lia   **6**

FAMILY MEMBERS

Leon Mandrake's grandfather on his mother's side, John Wagner, was a ship salvager and merchant in Sydney, Cape Breton, Nova Scotia. He married Mary Jane Moore in 1867. They lost two baby girls to whooping cough before their son, William, was born. Then when Mary died two years later of consumption, John remarried to Rebecca MacDonald. This marriage produced five children: John, Mildred , Emily, Harriet, and (Al)bert. Shortly after the railroad to British Columbia was completed in 1887, John and his son, William, then aged sixteen, travelled the 4000 miles across the North American continent by water, train, and stage coach to New Westminster, B. C. They may have travelled with John's brothers or his wife's brothers as well. In two years, when they had settled in, John sent for the rest of the family to join them out west. Rebecca, aged thirty-four, was willing to make the long journey with five children aged six to fourteen years. However, twelve-year-old daughter, Mildred, refused to come unless their grandmother, Annie MacDonald (of Scottish descent), was sent money to travel too. So, reluctantly, by all accounts, John sent tickets for his perhaps sharp-tongued mother-in-law as well. Eventually, John and his brothers went to sea as fishermen. Unfortunately, John was declared missing at sea in 1897, and believed lost by 1901.

(In 1979, the family found a tombstone in the graveyard of a mission in Santa Barbara, California that read "Michael MacDonald, native of Sydney, Nova Scotia, died 1910 at 76"; a man nine years older than John. Could he have been Rebecca's brother?) The eldest daughter, Mildred, an attractive blonde by all accounts, at age thirty-two began working in the New Westminster post office and eventually bought a house (307 Carnarvon Street) for the family. She never married and supported the family all her life. In those days, many women often had to accept jobs of laundry, sewing, or cooking with little hope of high wages. She and her mother had worked as seamstresses. As we know, the youngest sister, Harriet (Hattie), married and then divorced twice, coming home with one and then two young sons. The bedridden brother Bert, was unable to work for the rest of his life. Brother John was an eccentric, creative inventor, who undoubtedly passed on some of his talent to his nephew, Leon. Sister Emily married Alfred Poingdestre and had three children; two daughters and a son: Joyce, Evelyn, and Mervyn. Later, her marriage failed. Her husband took the eldest daughter, Joyce, leaving Emily to raise the two younger children on her own.

Years later, Aunty Mil paid for business training for Evelyn, who then worked in the Westminster Building on Columbia Street until she met and married Jeff Godson. They moved to Port Alberni where they kept the lighthouse for many years. Unfortunately, her brother, Mervyn, at age twenty-two, was struck and killed by a motorcycle he was filming in Chilliwack, B.C. The Godsons adopted a son who ran away at sixteen. He later resurfaced after his father's death to visit Evelyn, then in her seventies, with photos of her grandchildren in Ontario. That same year, the truck he was driving jack-knifed and he died. The two sisters, Evelyn and Joyce, were reunited late in life. At Evelyn's funeral, Leon Mandrake was very surprised to meet his cousin, Joyce, again after so many years.

Leon went on the road as early as sixteen years of age. Over the years, he kept in contact with his family between visits by writing to his mother and grandmother. It was after his grandmother, Rebecca Wagner, died that he started to find letters hidden in various places in his magic luggage. The first, in his trunk, was a lengthy letter as usual, (both she and Leon were philosophers at heart). She often added a gold sovereign between the pages. He found this first letter during his divorce from his first wife, Narda, and it was a great comfort. Leon said the strange thing was that every time he found another letter from his grandmother, the contents seemed to address the very issues he was facing in life. It was almost as if she were watching over him, giving him advice and comfort when he needed it most.

King George V gold Sovereigns (1911 to 1932) were minted throughout the British Empire, including Australia with a smaller number in Canada. These coins are only the size of today's nickel. It is difficult to determine the buying power of a sovereign in the 1930s, but we heard Leon say that you could rent a room for the night for fifty cents. He suggested to his boys to always have a silver dollar (or equivalent) in your pocket, so you had a room over your head and breakfast for the next morning.

THE REAL MANDRAKE THE MAGICIAN

Aunty Mildred (1879 - 1967) in later years in the kitchen of 307 Carnarvon St., New Westminster with Mandrake's three sons, the eldest Lonny, Ronny (forefront) and Kim (background) about 1955. One photo now lost to us showed her in her fashionable white suit at the post office staff gathering among a virtual sea of male workers; she may have been the only female on a staff of at least fifty at that time.

Leon's mother, Harriet, and his Uncle Billy at the store on Grosvenor Road, Surrey, B. C.

Carl,
Mandrake's Older Brother

While living in New Westminster, B.C., Leon's mother, Harriet Wagner, had met Alfred Jackson, the brother of the then-mayor of the city. They fell in love and married in about 1905. The Jacksons travelled a lot, often from one race track to another, since Alfred had a great interest in gambling. After the birth of their second child, Carl, in 1907, Harriet grew weary of handling two small children on the road. She wanted a more stable environment for the boys.

They were in San Francisco in 1906 when the earthquake hit the city. She was trapped in an elevator for quite some time. After the death of her eldest son, who had fallen down a flight of stairs, Harriet was distraught and blamed the itinerant lifestyle for the accident. She left Alfred and moved back to New Westminster with her younger son, Carl, to live with her mother and sister, Mildred, at 307 Carnarvon Street. The Jacksons eventually divorced.

In 1909 or 1910 Harriet remarried a professional chef working in New Westminster; Arthur Giglio. They moved with Carl to Arthur's hundred acres on Orcas Island, Washington and worked the farm. Their son, Leon, was born on April 11, 1911. Unfortunately, the marriage failed; the couple divorced and Harriet returned again to New Westminster with Carl and Leon. The two boys grew up together in New Westminster, which became known as the Royal City. In 1932, Leon was on the road performing when he was called home for the funeral of his brother, Carl. The body of Carl Jackson, aged twenty-five, was found in Robert Burnaby Park, a twenty-minute streetcar ride from New Westminster. His mouth and face had been eaten away by hydrochloric acid (prussic acid). The police suggested he may have committed suicide. Perhaps Carl had borrowed money from vicious money lenders who had made an example of him to scare others into prompt repayment. Carl had had a girlfriend who had become pregnant. He had wanted to marry the girl, but she wanted to go away and have the baby adopted. Even though he was only a mill worker, he was able to give her a large sum of money to do this. A short time later she returned, the money spent, saying she had reconsidered and wanted more money for a wedding dress. Eventually, Carl learned she had left town with an old boyfriend. One wonders if Carl had even been the father. Harriet, his mother, however, felt she was obliged to help the girl financially when the baby was born. Leon perhaps believed he could have helped his brother, if he had been home instead of performing on the road. To his last days, he couldn't bear to speak of the incident.

The newspaper printed an article by an investigative reporter who pointed out that the empty acid bottle had been thrown so far away in the brush that it was obvious it had been thrown by his assailant – Carl would have been unable, in such excruciating pain, to have thrown it himself. Also the reporter found the acid purchase was made at a Burnaby pharmacy by an unknown man. Carl's photo was not recognized as the purchaser.

However, the police still labeled it as suicide and did not investigate.

Leon's Uncle Billy

William Wagner was the son of John Wagner by a first marriage in Cape Breton, Nova Scotia, Canada. He was several years older than his three step-sisters, Mildred, Harriet, and Emily, and his two step-brothers, John and Bert.

William came to New Westminster, British Columbia with the family and made a life for himself. He helped to build the first pier in White Rock and, for years, he ran a convenience store out of the house he built himself from lumber and stained glass windows from the demolished Port Mann hotel at 14106 Grosvenor Road in Whalley, Surrey, B.C. He was a kind-hearted man who often let the local customers, down on their luck, defer payment on groceries they needed. The old-fashioned cash register he used (the highest amount available to be rung in was $4.99), is still in the Mandrake family. Over the years, he stored loose change in old tobacco cans and buried quite a few of them in the garden. One evening, two young men held him up, robbing the store of a pittance, no doubt, and clubbing the dear eighty-year-old man on the head with a gun. Uncle Billy died in hospital of a brain hemorrhage several days later.

The Farm

In his late teens, Leon lived with his dad on the Orcas Island farm for a short time. Arthur Giglio enrolled him in a business course, where Leon won interstate typing speed contests. But when Arthur suggested Leon marry the farmer's daughter next door and take up farming, Leon could not give up the show business he loved.

When Arthur died and Leon inherited the hundred acres, he hired a couple to look after the farm while he was in the hospital recovering for months from his car accident. When he visited later, the couple pointed out they had a son in a wheelchair and finances were tight, so Leon, the kind-hearted man he was, waived the rent. He learned later that the pair were both working at other jobs and letting the farm run to ruin. A lot of the original farm animals were gone when he finally dismissed them. Eventually, he could not cope with the farm while on the road and he finally sold the property. Today, it is considered prime real estate. (photo Harriet & Arthur's farm)

MARRIAGES

Narda

Leon Mandrake's first wife, Lola Narda Wilson, born in 1921, was one of twelve children living on their parents' farm in Iowa. Narda was of high-school age during the 1930s, the Depression of the "Dirty Thirties," a time when families were struggling. One day she was called into the principal's office. She had given out the school's phone number for personal calls. The principal said that they didn't mind a call or two (knowing there was no phone on her farm), but there were too many calls and this must stop. He had heard that she sometimes fell asleep in class and he was concerned. Narda had advertised herself as a dancer and these were all business calls. She said her family needed the money that she could bring in by dancing, and if she couldn't continue to use the school's phone she would have to leave school in order to find some other employment. She explained she taught dance lessons after school and then often had three dance shows a night, seven, nine, and eleven p.m. (and often had to wash siblings' dirty diapers when she got home – didn't mention that). The principal said he had no idea she had such "a lot on her plate", knew she was an A student and hated to see her education cut short, so the phone arrangement carried on.

Narda used to watch old movies starring Fred Astair and Ginger Rogers and tried to learn their dance steps. Then a school friend was learning dance from her vaudevillian dancer uncle and she passed what she learned on to Narda who loved to tap dance and practiced till she was so adept that she got a job teaching dance to youngsters after school.

One day she entered an amateur dance contest. She had no family to cheer her on like the others and her makeshift costume was no match for those of the well-to-do children competing. Apparently the vote was by volume of audience approval and there was no one there to applaud Narda. Discouraged, in the dressing room, she was surprised when she was summoned to speak with the hotel manager who had arranged the contest. He said she was a natural born dancer and had more talent than all of the contestants put together. He wanted to manage her career and she signed on.

Some time later, family life was disrupted when Narda's older sister eloped with a handsome, athletic chap who happened to be one-eighth African American. In those days, eighty years ago, prejudice was rampant. The whole family was shunned. One of the girls was suddenly fired from her job and the siblings in school found that their teachers would not speak to them. Finally, when the regular customers stopped buying their farm products, the family moved to another town.

By the age of sixteen, Narda was on the road working as a tap and Hawaiian dancer, eventually using live doves in her act. Later, her younger sister, Maja, played drums and joined her.

Narda remembers:

"I was down to my very last money when I came to town. I didn't have enough for a hotel room. I went to the nicest club to find work, but the owner seemed hesitant. So I said that if I couldn't fill the club that night, he didn't have to pay me. I went out and bought large paper sheets and paints with my precious few cents and made posters advertising the show. I put them up all over town. And, that night, the place was packed. I was paid and hired for the next two weeks."

Narda was a seasoned act by the time she met Leon Mandrake in Winslow, Arizona in 1939. They were married in 1940 in Seattle. She took her second name, Narda, as a stage name. The Mandrake show featured her with Mandrake's doves that she trained to fly out over the audience and land on her costume. Together, the Mandrakes played the best houses in many large cities including New York, Miami, and Chicago. Narda's artistic talents were an asset to the show as well. On the west coast, the show worked the circuit down into California. They lived in Hollywood for a while, playing in the prestigious Orpheum Theatre. Narda took advantage of being close to the internationally famous ballet dancer, Ruth St. Dennis, whom she had always admired, and asked to take advanced lessons from her. St. Dennis agreed when Leon said he would type out her autobiography in return for the lessons.

Narda, always an independent spirit, wanted equal billing with Mandrake, not to be just an added attraction. This may have caused difficulties in their marriage. By 1946, Narda had left and they were divorced. She later married Mandrake's old friend, Roy Benson, a comedy magician out of New York. This marriage lasted only a few years. Narda continued to perform with her sister in Cuba, the Dominican Republic, and even down into South America, where they played in Peru and Argentina. Then sadly her dancing career ended with a foot injury. Eventually she married Eugene Pohl and helped with his business for many years in Kentucky. Because they had vacationed in Mexico over the years, she decided, after he passed, to live there permanently.

She has fascinating stories to tell: "We had rented one of the celebrity homes in Beverly Hills since it was cost effective for a show troupe. It was a beautiful palatial house owned by the renowned radio and TV broadcaster, world traveller and author, Lowell Thomas who at the time was hosting The Wild Kingdom TV show..I used to take the train with my cages of trained doves to shows I had booked. One day, the wife of Lowell Thomas, our landlord, came for a visit and we talked so long, I was too late to catch the train for my engagement. I had to drive. Turns out, if I had caught that train, I surely would have died. There was an accident, a collision, and the whole back of the train was demolished. Because of the doves, I always sat in the caboose.

"I was staying in an apartment in Miami, Florida, taking bookings for my act. I had an engagement lined up with the Lyons club or so I thought. But as it got closer to the date of the show, I hadn't received a confirmation or even heard from them at all. So I contacted them. They were most surprised to hear from me because they thought I was dead. Apparently, I wasn't the only exotic female dancer with doves in the country as I had thought. There had been another one living in MY APARTMENT BUILDING and she had died two weeks before. When the Lyons agent saw the obituary and the right address, he naturally assumed it was me. I'd like someone to figure out the odds on that one!"

When Lon and Linda Mandrake flew to Mexico in 2018 to finally meet Narda aged 97, in person, They were impressed with her wit and saucy comebacks reminiscent of a Mae West character. She said all the girls were falling for Mandrake's hypnotic green eyes. When a friend said to tease her, "And what about you?"

she looked at him for a moment and then said, "Absolutely!" She made us laugh a lot, came out to the airport to greet us, and showed us wonderful hospitality.

One of her best stories showed how well she trained and looked after her birds. "I used to take my birds out for fresh air and exercise. One time, in Reno, my lead bird, a fan-tailed pigeon, flew out over the Truckee River and perched on a rock amid the ice flows of March. He couldn't come to me when I called him because his wings were getting wet from the water splash-ing up on him. Birds can't fly with wet wings. To save him I jumped into the water and swam out to him, putting him in the neck of my shirt. We made it back to the hotel dripping wet and I dried him off and kept him warm; in an hour we were both fine."

When I admired her professional quality stone sculpture of a beautiful sea goddess she had done several years earlier, and said I didn't have her artistic talent, she said, "Never say you can't do something – give it a try!"

GENII The CONJUROR'S MAGAZINE — March 1951 Vol. 15 No. 7

MANDRAKE THE MAGICIAN

Leon and Narda Mandrake

THE REAL MANDRAKE THE MAGICIAN

How Leon and Velvet Met

After Narda left the show, Leon went to the theatrical agency in Chicago to look for a replacement assistant. The agent recommended Louise Salerno, a petite brunette, who had stage experience and had worked with a magician. Leon was unsure because he had been thinking along the lines of a statuesque blonde. However, when a meeting was arranged, it was revealed that Louise had worked for a year with the great and famous magician, Blackstone. Mandrake agreed to hire her for the two-week gig until the agent could line her up with a repertory company. To this day Velvet (Louise) giggles, "I signed on for two weeks and stayed forty-seven years!"

Louise's parents had been in show business. Frank Salerno, a child prodigy on the accordion, immigrated as a teenager from Sicily. He had his own radio show for years, and Louise's mother sang on stage as well. Even her grandmother supported Louise's dance lessons. The dance students often performed in stores on Saturdays in Beloit, Wisconsin. Later, in senior high and afterwards, Louise joined a repertory group that toured in several states and performed five different plays. "I used to memorize pages and pages," Velvet remembers. She then worked for a year as an assistant for the great magician Blackstone. It was a highlight for her, but her first love was live drama.

Leon agreed to pick Louise up the following night for the drive to the first performance of the tour. Mrs. Salerno knew nothing of this magician employer and was apprehensive about her daughter's new job. And to make things worse, Mandrake was running late. "I don't know about this, Louise. The first time to come to the house and he's half an hour late." Luckily, Mrs. Salerno had to go out and while she was away, Leon showed up. If her mother had been there to greet the young chap, Louise may never have gone on tour with Mandrake.

They set off on the winter highways only to skid on black ice and lose control of the vehicle. The car flipped upside down in a field. Unhurt, they climbed out, deciding what to do. "The show must go on," was the sentiment they both lived by so Mandrake walked back to a gas station they had passed earlier while Louise stayed with the car, with the valuable costumes and stage props.

Velvet (Louise) remembers: "I was standing by the car in the cold, thinking: *Oh, Mama would have a fit if she knew what I'm doing right now.*"

She and Leon made the show on time and probably never told Mama about the accident.

When asked if she and Leon were married in a simple ceremony, Velvet's answer was, "Simple is right. We were married at six o'clock, by eight we were doing the show."

And to the question, what was your schedule like on the road? Velvet's answer:

"Our schedule was really hectic, especially in the years between 1948 to 1955. We hardly had a day off. I was petite and didn't show that I was pregnant until about six months. I wore costumes with draping sleeves and I learned how to fit into illusions without hurting my tummy. Then, one of the girls would replace me on stage for the last three months. I remember I was back at work three weeks after Ronny was born."

Velvet with the Blackstone magic show (seated third from left)
Below is Velvet's mother, Betty Salerno. much later with great granddaughter, Katrina

THE REAL MANDRAKE THE MAGICIAN

Leon and Velvet Mandrake

Velvet's Parents

Frank Salerno, a native of Palermo, Sicily, Italy, was the youngest of three boys. He was of small build, while his brothers were much taller, bigger men. In those days of hard times and scarce food, Frank always believed he was small because he got little to eat. But because his daughter, Velvet, inherited his petite stature, we realize today it was a genetic factor.

Frank was a child musical prodigy, excelling at playing the accordion at a very early age. He was asked to perform at weddings, and he often had to walk many miles to get there with only a loaf of bread and a bit of cheese for the two-day trip back home. He always remembered passing the shrines for dead people along the road (victims of the Sicilian gangsters in the area).

At the age of sixteen, Frank crossed the Atlantic to join his brothers in America. With his cousin, Lawrence, he developed a musical show and they called themselves the Salerno brothers. When Frank met and married Elizabeth (Betty) Strucuzza, she joined them as a singer. They ran their own radio show out of Chicago for years. Frank even designed and made his own accordion.

When he was working in a nightclub owned by Al Capone, he noticed people being taken out back, and he heard gun shots and saw that people were disappearing. He got so nervous witnessing these crimes that he finally said he wanted to leave the club. When a Capone henchman said, "Are you going to let him go?" and showed his gun, the manager said, "Yes, Frank's a pisano, he's from Sicily, he's fine."

Frank lost no time in moving Betty and his daughter, Velvet, far away to California.

In California, Velvet took dance lessons and excelled at acting. There, Betty had their home proudly displayed in *Home and Garden* magazine with Frank's beautiful garden of flowers and fruit trees adding to its charm. He ran an accordion school at this time with more than thirty students.. When Frank suddenly wanted to return to Chicago, Betty was heart-broken to leave her beautiful house and the California she loved. She said, at that time there were miles and miles of orange groves scenting the air in spring. By the time Velvet had graduated high school, the Salernos had divorced.

Frank never remarried but eventually lived in California again and then Washington to be close to his daughter and his grandchildren. They remember the tasty donuts he always brought when he visited and the wonderful music he played and recorded for them. Betty remarried Scottie Grace, a retired Marine, in Chicago, where they ran an ice cream and soda shop called The Sip and Dip. When Leon and Velvet were not allowed to enroll their children in regular school, because they were travelers and not paying taxes in that state, they had Betty and Scottie home-school them for a short time.

Lon remembers, "We often got a milkshake before we did our homework."

The Graces eventually moved to California where Scottie worked in the post office. The children have fond memories of "Uncle" Scottie and Gram. (see photo page 85)

A FAMILY ON THE ROAD

Velvet remembers:

"We managed to take the children along with us most of the time on the road. It meant so much to me to have them with me. And they were well behaved. We'd get into a new town, check into the hotel, and ask the desk if they could recommend a babysitter, just for the few hours when we were performing. Sometimes we took the children to the theatre with us. I had Lonny, Ronny, and Kim. I told them that they had to be very quiet backstage, and they played and watched and were really no trouble. They played games on the floor of the stretch limousine and stayed quiet in restaurants if we were talking to business associates. I think they knew that if they wanted to be with us, they had to be good.

"I remember one time sharing a dressing room with other performers and over- hearing this one woman's husband saying to her, 'What do you mean we can't have a family if you're performing? Look at Velvet Mandrake with three children on the road.' The woman snarled back, 'YOU LOOK!' and stormed off."

It was decided at one point that baby Ronald would stay with his grandmother, Betty Salerno, for a awhile. She travelled with him by train from Florida back to her home in Chicago. Betty was delighted to be able to care for the little fellow while her daughter and Leon performed in the Florida nightclubs.

Lon (Leon Junior) remembers:

"I don't know if it was the change from hot weather to cooler that did it, but Ronny got really sick. He came down with pneumonia. I think they almost lost him. After that, Mum and Dad liked to keep us with them as much as possible."

The Mandrake family created a permanent base on Grosvenor Road in Surrey in about 1958. Leon began extensive renovations on Uncle Billy's house, which he had inherited, and the children enrolled in the elementary school. When the summer holidays came, the family set out on a road trip down the coast to California, performing previously arranged engagements along the way. Lon remembers it was an adventure each summer to be travelling with their parents. "In a Sacramento resort, we all had private lessons and learned to swim."

One of the family's favorite locations was near home, Harrison Hot Springs in B.C. It is a beautiful spot, a resort and spa built on a lake nestled in the mountains. The Mandrakes performed many times in the elegant "Copper Room" dinner and dance area overlooking one of the outdoor pools. The discovery of the hot spring water had been made in the 1800s. A lake fisherman happened to fall over-board just at the spot where the amazingly hot spring water bubbles up from the bottom of the lake. They have to cool the water down to use it in the hot tubs. Now the resort is crowded with people from all over the world, especially with

Europeans who feel right at home in the mountainous setting.

During their engagement the Mandrakes were given one of the large private cabins and passes for the wonderful dining. In those days, there were a lot of programs for children with fulltime coordinators like horseback riding, arts and crafts, hiking, sand castles on the sandy beach, and of course the hot tubs and swimming.

Another favorite stop was Hoberg's Resort and Spa at Clear Lake on Cobb Mountain in California. The lake is the oldest lake in North America at half a million years old. Unfortunately, the extensive resort burned to the ground in a forest fire in 2015. The Mandrake show was always popular at Hoberg's. Lon remembers staying in the fashionable cabins with names like "Oak" and "Cedar" after the many trees on the property and enjoying the swimming and hiking. He was nearly old enough to be curious about the teen dances held in the open air. And the food was outstanding. The resort with its golfing and waterskiing, which stood for over a hundred years, will be missed by a great many people.

Velvet's father was living in Santa Cruz, California for a time. Lon recalls visiting him there where the family enjoyed the wonderful weather and the fabulous boardwalk on the beach. On one visit Lon, the eldest, maybe fifteen at the time, made an interesting discovery. California girls were more outgoing and friendly compared to the reserved Canadian girls back home. This was a delight to a naturally shy boy. Lon says he met many children of entertainers on the road and a lot of them were surprisingly shy.

Velvet says:

"Most of the time we got great babysitters and had no trouble. However, there was one girl in Chicago who was a disappointment. We were doing an afternoon show and so we left her in the hotel room with three-year-old Lonny and two-year-old Ronny, who was young enough to be in a carriage. The girl might have been fine if she had stayed in the hotel, but she decided to take the two boys to a nearby park. Somehow, she lost Lonny. She spent an hour looking all over for him and then she went back to the hotel and did nothing but cry and wait for us to return. By the time she had confessed to us that she had lost our son, three-year-old Lonny had been alone in the city of Chicago for several hours. We were horrified so much time had been wasted. Leon phoned the police right away and, thank Heavens, Lonny was there at the police station. Someone had found him and given him to a policeman. When we got to the station, there he was, sitting on the chief's desk, eating an ice cream cone and smiling up at us."

For longer tours the Mandrakes hired a housekeeper.

Lon remembers:

"There was one housekeeper who really was terrible. I mean, we were teenagers by then. Mom and Dad had gone on tour (a week in Oregon) and we had this older lady. She was well respected by her church and came recommended, especially since she had had twelve children of her own. Right away, she said the TV was not allowed and the radio was not to be on unless we were listening to a religious program. Listening to music was really important to us at that age. She used to sing hymns at the top of her lungs all day long. But it was the food that was the biggest problem. She served us plain spaghetti one night (remember we were used to Mum's Italian sauces), and none of us ate much of it. This infuriated her, so she wrapped it all up and served it again the next night and the next night. All the time, we were watching her eat a plate full of pork chops, mashed potatoes, and gravy, and wondering why we couldn't have some of that. 'Waste not, want not' was her motto. Mum and Dad were really shocked about her when they finally got home.

"And then there was the sitter in Hawaii who brought her own two girls with her and stayed overnight. She put us all to bed and then started to drink. She was quite drunk by the time her husband arrived at the door. He came in, and they got into an argument, which turned into a downright brawl. She must have cut him with a kitchen knife because he left abruptly. In the morning, there was quite a lot of blood on the kitchen floor."

Velvet remembers:

"This one hotel didn't allow animals; it was late, we needed a room near the theatre so Leon hid the doves, the rabbits, and our duck within several of the illusions. The animals were really quiet. We just walked them right past the front desk along with the other props. I loved having the kids with me. It was work, but I was young and didn't mind. I often took them to a park in the afternoon, to have a good play and get some fresh air and exercise. Then I'd feed them, give the sitter her instructions, and then dress for the show.

"One night, I remember we had a big show, with full orchestra and a packed house. At the end, the audience really liked us and they came up on stage and presented me with a bouquet of red roses. We took our bows and we felt like the toast of the town. Then heading back to the hotel room, I went to relieve the sitter while Leon organized back stage. I rolled up my sleeves and thought, what a contrast, as I spent the rest of the evening washing out poopy diapers in the bathroom sink," (and she laughed reliving the memory).

Lon remembers his unusual childhood:

"I went to five different schools in the first grade. [This didn't seem to deter him from graduating from UBC with a Bachelor of Science fifteen years later.] I went to school in Hawaii in 1957. I was, let's see, eight years old. That's grade three. We were there six months. Every morning, we sang the American anthem. Kids are really indoctrinated there compared to Canada. And we noticed how the text books that said Captain Cook was a fearless, heroic adventurer were looked upon differently by the Hawaiian natives. They believed he was a ruthless man who was eventually murdered by the native people he had exploited. The school had huge glass windows, so that you could see nature outside. Most of the teachers were Japanese. I made friends of many different nationalities there, and we had great fun exploring the old hospital that was, no doubt, out of bounds. Nevertheless, they called me a 'Howlee' [white boy]. I loved Hawaii; it was so unspoiled then. We had a mango tree right outside the kitchen window. I was just the right age to be there.

"Meanwhile, my parents were producing a large show called *The Melting Pot* for the opening [1957] of the Kaiser [Geodesic] Dome. My dad added to his performance by bringing in Polynesian dancers, a marionetteer, a comedian, a singer, and a guest magician, Andrew Park. Dad said he wanted to give back to the Hawaiian people for welcoming him so warmly, and so he did a free afternoon show for children – thousands came for a full house. Mum and Dad entertained at many venues, including the travelling carnival, which toured the islands and a Honolulu night club called The Pearl City Tavern and Monkey Bar where Don Ho was early in his career. Its name belied the grand nature of its huge and elegant Japanese-style dining room, with floor shows nightly and waitresses in kimonos. The Monkey Bar was world famous for its live monkeys in a glass cage behind the bar and ceramic monkey mugs in the large café. The Mandrakes played there in early 1957. It was open from 1939 to 1993 when the business closed."

THE REAL MANDRAKE THE MAGICIAN

Velvet recalls one nightclub owner, a white woman, very wealthy, who kept an extremely handsome, younger Hawaiian man as her manager. He wore very expensive clothes and drove a fast, new car. Then one day, he took an interest in one of the waitresses. Within a day, he was stripped of his job and fancy car and was left in his nice clothes as a beach bum again. "I had never seen anything so fast," says VVelvet. "She had put nothing in his name; he was completely ruined.

"In those days entertainers never admitted to being married. It added to the mystique and appeal to be single. So, I was always billed as Miss Velvet. When Leon and I married and we were expecting our first child, I concealed my pregnancy with the draping sleeves of my costume. We had just finished a show and sat down at a club table. The clubs liked us to mix with some of the guests, so I accepted a dance with a man from the audience. When our bodies touched, the baby gave a huge kick. You should have seen the look on his face! No one dreamed I was nearly six months pregnant. He went back to his table and whispered and whispered to his friends. I was so glad that was our closing night and we could leave in the morning."

Lonny went to school [grade one] in Fairbanks, Alaska. He remembers how all the children were picked up by school buses and delivered to the school grounds. One day, coming off the bus, he was suddenly surrounded by several husky dogs. He started to run from them, but they sprang upon him and knocked him down. Growling and snarling and baring their teeth, the large dogs started pulling at his little red-leather cap with the ear flaps. Because of the chin strap, they had to really pull in opposite directions to finally get it off his head. It must have smelled like an animal skin that they felt obliged to attack. Three of them fought for the prize, ripping it to shreds. Finally, the teacher came out to greet the children and rescue frightened Lonny. Nevertheless, the family later enjoyed playing with a neighbor's husky pups; Lon says, "They were lots of fun." On the other hand, he has never liked hats.

Leon and Velvet's Family

Lon (science teacher and mentalist), Ron (magician), Kim (musician) and Jill (Geelia) writer and librarian

At home in B.C., Mandrake developed a board game he called Esper to teach his children memory and mental skills. The game gave you challenges like: memorize fifty objects on a tray, turn your back while one is removed, and then say which one is missing. There were prizes for success – a silver dollar, a movie, or an outing with Mum and Dad. The living room was busy with books, chess sets, puppets, and puzzles like Chinese puzzle boxes, while the office featured magic memorabilia, show photos, and Leon's own full-wall filing system for cards, sponge balls, ropes, and coins, all the things that drive magicians' wives crazy. Many tools and paints were well organized too. And in the closet, there was a riot of color and sparkles from all those wonderful show costumes. The workroom was the grandchildren's favorite because the Egyptian mummy case (used in *The Beachcombers* TV show) sat in the corner and they loved to play hide and seek in it for fun.

Our daughter, Katrina, says:

"It would have been marvelous if we could have disappeared as an added advantage in our game, however, we were unsure of how the magic worked, and we triple-checked every inch in trying to figure it out. The mystery was the magic; to be shown would have destroyed that, which all the grandchildren are thankful for. 'How do YOU think it's done?' being the answer to how the illusions work. Instead, all the attempts to figure it out inspired creative thinking. It would have been a disappointment to have the mystery finally revealed, the magic and amazement of it lost. Only when ready to learn and pass that joy to others, was one taught. Mandrake invented countless magic tricks of his own, as well as his own variations of existing ones, that not only baffled the audience but also other magicians as well.

"Mandrake, in his love of magic, was always performing on stage and off, and also long after he had retired from doing shows. Many of the neighborhood kids would come knocking on the door to his home on Grosvenor Road asking if he could show them a few magic tricks and make them balloon animals. It didn't matter how busy he happened to be at that moment, or how often different groups of kids would come knocking, he welcomed them at the door with a smile of delight, the doorframe becoming his stage."

Lon recalls:

"Once I brought a new date home to have coffee and meet the family. Dad greeted her warmly then said, 'Lonny, I've been working on this all morning, let me know how it looks.' Okay, Dad, I said as I went into the kitchen to put the water on to boil. I was gone a very short time. When I came back to the living room, my date had vanished. Apparently, she had suddenly bolted out the front door. Dad had floated a skull across the room and scared the wits out of her."

Linda Remembers:

Originality was always Mandrake's forte. He was sometimes helped by talented, creative builders, costumers, and promotional people, but the original magic ideas came from him. Often at his house for dinner, Lon and the kids and I would be greeted with new illusions he imagined even as he whipped up a tasty side salad to complement Velvet's roast dinner. There was often an extra mouth to feed at this table, maybe a hopeful amateur learning at the knee of the master (and sometimes later denying it). Velvet always came up with a delicious dinner and never made a complaint as Leon spoke warmly of throwing another potato in the pot. 'What's mine is yours" was the feeling he gave. And it was genuine. One chap, I was told, stayed six weeks…Velvet's a great cook.

I understand that Leon's mother, Harriet, provided a strong moral upbringing; she later became quite religious. It was she who insisted that young Leon run, not walk, to the butcher to pay a rare outstanding bill. Later, Leon instilled in his children the importance of honesty, of paying debts first, of saving a percentage of your wage for a rainy day, of giving full value. So, if Leon happened to pick your pocket on stage as you prepared to return to your seat, your wallet was never in safer hands.

I believe that my husband Lon has inherited some of Mandrake's magnetic personality – that is, his innate ability to command attention both on and off stage. When Mandrake entered a room and spoke, all eyes were on him. I analyzed it as best I could: eye contact, volume, tone of voice, emphasis, timing. Yet, behind it all was that fascinating personality twinkling behind magnetic green eyes. People liked his magic, but it was the man they loved.

Mandrake's philosophy of life kept him happy. Can you imagine supporting a family of six (and often more) on the road? Most of us are weary after a short holiday with the kids. It was Leon who coined the phrase for a show segment, "Every day's a holiday." I'm sure if someone had stolen something from him, he would have said, "Well, he must have needed it very badly, prob-ably more than me." He wasn't materialistic, although he liked to wear dramatic suits and always that trademark boutonniere flower, often a rose or carnation, on his lapel; indeed he often signed his name with a sketch of a flower. Somehow vibrant patterns and bright colors suited his personality. He often laughed and said that sometimes we are eating steak and sometimes beans, but you're welcome to both. Leon was a universal thinker, neither prude nor rounder, a man of intelligence and humor – a flower child long before the term became popular.

Leon always said how pleased he was that I'd joined the family; that Lon and I had found each other, and that I enjoyed the mentalism and backed Lon's interest in it. When I heard how Leon admired master magician Howard Thurston, mostly because of his creativity and the fact that he always played the part of the magician on and off stage, I felt that Leon was really describing himself.

Leon once said at the end of a show, "As you go through life, the only thing of value you take with you are memories." My memories of him warm my heart."

THE SHOW MUST GO ON

"What could go wrong, would go wrong" is the essence of Murphy's Law. This was occasionally the case with performances over the years, no doubt. Below are some true family adventures:

Mandrake in the Cold

Recreated by Linda

Perhaps he shouldn't have taken the left fork in the road. It was so dark and desolate in the desert between Las Vegas and Reno, especially this late at night.

Well, what could he do? The closing show had run until ten. Then it took a good hour to pack and collect his cheque. The manager of the club had bent his ear about staying on for another month, but he had already promised to open in Reno the next night. He'd have to drive his 1934 Ford coupe all night, catch a quick nap, and open by seven. There was never enough time it seemed. Perhaps he shouldn't have had the ham and eggs at the club; that had set him back a half an hour. Ham and eggs wouldn't be his choice of a last meal.

There wasn't any traffic at all. He hadn't passed another car in two hours. And it was getting cold. The car heater was on full blast.

Then it happened. Two loud bangs and the car swerved dangerously into the oncoming lane. He maneuvered back to the edge of the highway with limping wheels. When he opened the car door, the cold hit his body like the draft from a freezer. He saw right away there was not one but two flat tires. Feeling the cold of the metal handle ache into his hand, he opened up the trunk. Only one spare and...he discovered with dismay, it was flat.

He glanced up and down the highway in vain. Nothing. No one. How long would he have to wait for someone to come along and give him a lift into Reno? Then a dreadful thought crossed his mind: what if he were no longer on the main highway? A side road could be deserted for how long?

At least he could see by the light of the moon. The full orb shone down seeming to freeze everything below it. His breath hung in the air, as he looked through the jumble of suitcases and props for gloves. He always travelled light and had only one small case for personal items. In that, he found gloves but no hat. He glanced at his magician's top hat, secure in its case, but knew it wouldn't provide much warmth.

A gust of wind drove him back inside the vehicle. The temperature had dropped considerably, even in the short time that the heater had been off. He had read about men trying to survive extreme cold; about frozen, blackened toes and lost pieces of nose. The extremities were the first to go. He blew a hot breath into the wool gloves and the moist warmth felt good for a moment.

He grasped the icy steering wheel and turned the engine over. There was almost half a tank of gas. Could he limp along on the flats? He edged forward a short distance and realized he wouldn't make any speed and soon would be riding on the rims. The expense of repairing or buying two tires was bad enough without new rims. He'd wait it out. The gig in Reno was for a good friend; he'd played there so many times. He'd be forgiven for missing opening night. What else could he do?

He sat in the driver's seat with the heater as high as it would go for an hour before he realized he was running low on gas. He would ration it, turning it off until it was unbearable. In a few minutes, the cold stole in like a Ninja bent on death.

Sitting on the dampening seat, he rubbed his legs and slapped his arms to encourage circulation. His toes scrunched up inside the icy leather of his thin dress shoes, retreating from frostbite. He began to think he might not survive until dawn when surely someone would come by. He lit another cigarette, and looking at the red tip of it in the dark, decided he had to light a fire. He had a lighter and a spare can of lighter fluid. As he opened the car door, it creaked as if arthritic and the wind sucked away his body heat. He shivered; it was the body's defense against a temperature drop, he knew.

Using his lighter, he scanned the sandy ground for something to burn. Picking carefully among the rocks, worrying about desert scorpions, all he could find was shrub grass and a few twigs. He was reluctant to move too far from the car, in case someone came and drove by before he could flag them down. Then too, could there be wolves or cats looking for a meal in the dark? He returned to the front of the car, turned on the headlights, and lit his collected items. The momentary heat was wonderful on his hands and face, but it died out quickly. What else could he burn? His right ear suddenly twinged, and he slipped off his glove to warm it with his palm. The heat made it ache and itch. Frostbite. He covered the other ear for a moment then slipped the gloves back on. Opening up the back again, he looked for something to burn. Sponge balls, a wand, glass fish bowls, decks of cards… He couldn't burn his larger illusions; they were expensive and hard

to replace. And he had a three-week contract in Reno in the morning. If he made it to the morning. His legs felt stiff. His cheeks and eyes smarted with the cold. How low could a desert temperature drop? How long would it take for hypothermia to set in? He couldn't lose fingers; as a magician, his hands were his livelihood.

He grabbed up his wool cape, a magician's full-length cape that was so heavy it had a strong metal clasp at the neck to keep the shoulders in place. He wrapped it about him like a tent. And there, that left-over piece of felt he had used to re-cover a collapsible table would just wrap around his head. His ears felt the good of it right away. Perhaps the top hat on top of it all? He'd read that a lot of body heat is lost through your head. What an apparition he would be, flagging down another motorist. And he also knew people had been saved by hugging a tree when lost in a forest because it conserved body heat. But here there wasn't a tree for miles.

Then he saw it, the flat spare tire. Could he burn that? He knew tire fires burn a long time and give off a lot of black smoke. Maybe someone would see the smoke at dawn and it would be the saving of him. He gathered up more brush and dead grass and piled it into the center of the tire at a distance from the car. In spite of the cold, his resourcefulness and creative mind kicked in; he found a piece of rubber tubing and one of the fish bowls from the trunk. Sticking the tube into the gas tank, he sucked briefly on it to create a vacuum. Up came the gasoline into the bowl. And with the gasoline's superior explosion of heat, the rubber began to burn.

As the hours passed, he huddled beneath the wool cape on a box from the trunk as close to the fire as he dared. Covered in a greasy soot, he was nearly choking from the fumes. But he was surviving. He had to burn the two flat tires as well, before a pale dawn finally came. Then a roaring of a motor grew from a great distance off. Finally, he could see a pickup, solitary on the flat expanse of desert; a beacon of hope for a shivering magician.

The following adventures are recounted by Lon:

The Last Frontier

Often the owner of the night club Mandrake was performing in would ask that he circulate with the patrons after the show. In 1945, Leon was booked for three months at the Last Frontier Casino in Las Vegas. At the end of the run, he planned to return to Hollywood where he had broken the attendance record for a novelty act at the prestigious Orpheum Theatre. However, the casino wanted him to stay on with them and offered to double his salary. He would be paid half in cash and the other half would be credit at the gambling tables. They wanted him to circulate on the gambling floor and thus bring in high rollers who wanted to rub shoulders with the charismatic magician. With night after night of gambling, Mandrake soon had built up such a tab that he had to stay on for the rest of the year to pay off his debt. In the photo, he has put on a free afternoon show for the children of the casino staff. Narda is on Leon's left.

(1944 or 1945)

Don't Tell Me

In one nightclub in the mid-states, a regular patron watched the Mandrake show every night. Afterwards, he always sought out Leon to compliment him on his fine performance. He was a drinker and a talker, and night after night he would find Mandrake and bend his ear as he became more and more inebriated. Leon confided in Velvet that this fellow was making him nervous because he was beginning to spill confidences the drunker he got. As the engagement stretched into weeks, this man began to tell Leon he was a member of a notorious criminal group. Soon, he felt comfortable enough to reveal he was their hit man. Mandrake said he didn't want to hear it; he didn't want to know. But the fellow was in his cups and took no heed. So, Mandrake considered breaking his contract and moving on, worried the chap might wake up some morning, sober, and realize the magician knew too much and would have to be silenced. When the club, pleased with his performances, asked Mandrake to renew his contract, he and Velvet tactfully declined and got out of town in a hurry.

Only in Texas

In 1949 or 1950 the Mandrake show was performing in a nightclub in Dallas, Texas. Leon said that in those days Texas was a rather wild place. During the magic show, a drunk cowboy burst through the doors and rode his horse through the aisles, whooping it up. He grabbed the revolver from his holster and actually shot a bullet into the ceiling of the club. Apparently, everyone ducked for a few moments then gave their attention to the show again – the cowboy rode off and Mandrake carried on.

Balloons

Mandrake often made balloon animals during the show. There were the regular-size ones especially popular with children and then there were the giant balloon constructions that Mandrake had introduced. He twisted and tied balloons together to build things like a swan or a giraffe large enough for Velvet to sit on. In one promotional photo, she is riding a rocking horse.

The large balloon animals were very popular with adults as well as children. In one place, two grown men were fighting over one creation. They actually got into a fist fight over the balloon animal until Mandrake offered to solve the problem by making another creation for the second fellow. As they went away happy, someone told Leon that both men were running for public office.

The Rifle

The airport in Tokyo took one look at the rifle used in Mandrake's show and said it could not be taken into Japan. Leon protested that it was only a magic prop he needed for his performance, to no avail. The officials put the rifle in security and told the Mandrakes they could retrieve it when they left the country. Sometime later, back at the airport, they were running late to catch a plane for the Philippines. By the time they got the rifle out of security, their bags were already on board and there was no time to wrap the weapon. So, they took it along as carry on.

Landing in Manila, Leon gathered up the hand luggage and started across the tarmac to the airport building. Velvet followed behind with her purse and the rifle. Needless to say, the Philippine officials nearly did a flip when they saw the tiny brunette carrying a rifle. Today, they might have shut down the airport while they interrogated the apparent terrorist.

The Beatles

Leon and Velvet were performing at the Pacific National Exposition (PNE) in Vancouver, B.C. in August, 1964, as they had for so many seasons.

This year they were pleased to be placed on a stage in the Stadium Grounds. The previous year the performing area had been filled to capacity, all four shows a day, but the Stadium could hold a much larger audience. Tiered bleachers surrounded the stage and then metal fencing encircled the seating. There was a large swing gate in the center of the six-foot fence.

About five days into the seventeen days of Mandrake's performances, on August 22nd, the Beatles from England were scheduled to do the nine o'clock evening show. Organizers told Mandrake that he didn't have to remove all his equipment for the one show; he could just push it back behind the curtains. The British singers only needed the front part of the stage. Looking at the huge buzz saw with its dangerously sharp blade, Leon decided to move everything off stage into a storage area anyway for safety.

That night the bleachers were full to capacity. The show was a half an hour late starting. When Paul, John, George, and Ringo finally walked on stage, the crowd went wild. Girls shrieked and screamed. The crowd outside the fencing was unable to gain entrance through the locked gate. So, they started to climb the gate to get a better view of the famous Beatles. The foursome had performed a few songs (probably "I Wanna Hold Your Hand" for one), when suddenly the weight of so many people crashed the gate to the ground. The screaming crowd streamed down the aisle between the bleachers. The rest of the audience started to follow. The security guards saw the danger as 20,000 fans surged toward the stage. Before the boys could be torn apart for souvenirs like pieces of clothing or snips of hair, the guards rushed the Beatles out the back of the stage to a waiting car. Apparently, they were driven straight to the airport and were never seen in Vancouver again.

Next day, the Mandrake show resumed, as if nothing had happened. Luckily, the crazed mob wasn't injured by Mandrake's equipment.

No Laughs

Leon said that one time when he was performing, he noticed that he got great applause for his magic but not much reaction when he joked or used humorous one-liners. When he was talking to the manager afterward, he learned that the club was actually in Mexico and his audience didn't speak much English. In those days, the border was hardly noticeable; Leon had crossed it in the night and didn't know he'd left the United States.

Plush

Velvet and Leon were performing in the big tent at a carnival (was it in Hawaii?). One day, one of the carnies bragged that he was an excellent barker (one who calls out to bring people in). Leon finally agreed to let him advertise his big tent show. In a few minutes, he and Velvet heard, "Look! Look! Look! What's over here! Direct from Las Vegas, it's MANDREE AND PLUSH!!"

George

George Carl was an internationally famous acrobat and clown who worked with Mandrake for years. Popular in Europe, he was a favorite at the Crazy Horse in Paris and had done a command performance for Prince Rainier of Monaco. Always the practical joker, just for the fun of it sometimes George would do a prat fall (a fake trip) entering a restaurant – worried the staff like crazy. His Charlie Chaplin-like persona and trademark shrinking walk made him a favorite in clubs and on TV as well. One night he put his antics to good use when a problem arose with a recently-hired male assistant. The new man had started taking an extra bow outside the closed curtain after the Mandrakes had already bowed and retired as an end to their performance. Leon had told him not to do this several times but the chap kept doing it. So, George felt it necessary to take action: next night he grabbed the assistant by his ankles and neatly whipped him under the curtain, "disappearing" him instantly. The point was made clear, but still the man complained, "That man is going to kill me!"

Velvet with doves

Doves

Leon and Velvet had played the grand HotelVancouver on the corner of Georgia and Burrard Street with Dal Richards and his orchestra in the past. But this time, when the hotel called with an unusual request, they were surprised. Another performer, an amateurish fellow, had used doves in his act and lost several birds during the show. He had been unable to catch them as they had perched on the chandeliers hanging from the very high ballroom ceiling. The management provided a long ladder but every time the magician got close to a dove, it would take flight. Finally giving up, he had left town without his doves. The hotel management was in a panic since a formal dinner was planned for the ballroom that night. Mandrake said not to worry, he had lots of experience with doves; he'd be right there.

He used the long ladder too and had no trouble gathering up the birds. The secret? Doves won't fly in the dark. He turned off all the lights and used a flashlight to spot each stationary bird.

The Haunting

We had put the doves' cages in the hotel bathroom over the tub as usual. I was about fourteen years old and I was put in charge of the doves and rabbits for the afternoon while my parents and siblings were out shopping. Somehow, several doves escaped while I was caring for them (probably I left a cage door open). They flew out into the room and then, as I maneuvered to catch them, escaped out into the hallway. I chased them down the hall and, to my horror, saw them fly through the open grillwork of the elevator doors into the elevator shaft. When Dad got back, he was saying the manager of the hotel was concerned; several hotel guests had complained of ghostly noises in the hotel and wondered if Mandrake had haunted the place. I confessed my lapse of duty and Dad climbed onto the top of the elevator roof to retrieve the doves in the dark with a flashlight. It was the end of the haunting.

Busy Days

Example of the hectic show biz life (excerpt from Velvet's diary notes):

"Club in Seattle, take boys and Geelia (fourteen mos. old) to Chicago, drop off boys with Mama and Scottie. Geelia and I to meet Leon in Seattle then to Alaska to play Idle Hour – Xmas fire devastated for many reasons, three weeks at Elks Club in Anchorage then Geelia and I left Anchorage for Chicago to pick up boys then flew back to meet Leon in Seattle. We all drove down to Portland to meet four other acts and all flew to Hawaii for police promotional shows. Early Feb. the other acts returned to the States and we played everything including the new Kaiser Dome."

Narda with doves

Vent Act (Ventriloquism) Dummies

Leon found standing all evening (some shows were two hours long) rather difficult after the car accident that had weakened his leg. And so, he did his vent act between magical segments sitting on a chair center-stage. A ventriloquist is an entertainer who produces voice-sounds so that they seem to come from a source other than himself. He had three wooden dummies (three-foot full-body puppets); a White (Jerry), a Black (Sammy), and an Asian (Charlie), representing three races. As is often the case, Leon became very attached to his "children." He worked with them for years until a fire in a club in Phoenix, Arizona destroyed them all. His first wife, Narda, said that he was so upset with their loss that she made him a new one in a lovely Chinese costume. However, broken-hearted, Leon hardly used the new dummy at all. (Charlie seen at right)

First full color photo- new technology, 1955.

COSTUME

Vancouver's Ray Buchanan designed several of Velvet's costumes. I met him once at a "black and white" (dress code) party. A slim, well-dressed man, he complimented me on my shoes. I had worn a blocked black and white dress with black and white pumps. I bet most of the guests wouldn't have even noticed whether a pair of shoes were complementing an outfit or not. Last I heard, Ray, although not young, was travelling in Europe.

THE REAL MANDRAKE THE MAGICIAN

THE COMIC STRIP

Lee Falk, a prolific writer, artist, theatre director and producer first came up with the idea of Mandrake the Magician at the age of nineteen, while attending the University of Illinois. While on vacation in New York with his parents he showed his work to King Features and struck a deal. After graduation, he soon found a daily strip was too much work and hired fellow alumnus, Phil Davis to do the art work. They combined their talents – Lee Falk scripted the stories and Phil Davis did the art work for the first Mandrake comic in June, 1934.

In 1955, Leon Mandrake and Velvet were performing in St. Louis. Phil Davis caught the show and was greatly impressed with it. He waited to meet the stars after the performance to invite them and their children to see where the comic Mandrake was actually drawn. Lon remembers, at the age of seven, that Davis took them to his home studio where he autographed several poses of the comic character for Mandrake. After that meeting, Phil Davis' Mandrake looked more and more like the living Mandrake. The 1956 Dell Comic cover looks like a photograph of Leon with his green eyes, traditional attire, and even his large, square hand. They marveled that Narda's real name was coincidentally Narda like the woman in the comic strip. The artist and performer kept up a friendly correspondence over the years, a relationship that was a benefit to both.

(Note: The Wilson family must have had a fondness for exotic names for their daughters since Narda's younger sister was named Maja; she played the drum in the exotic dove dance routine and later worked on the Mandrake show as an assistant for several years, looking so much like Narda that people thought Narda could be in two different cities at once.)

On the following page is an illustration by Dell Comics issue 752, 1956, by King Features, of a comic book Mandrake remarkably similar to the real Mandrake.

Every good wish from one Magician to another.
Mandrake and
Phil Davis

PHIL M. DAVIS
1303 TOPPING ROAD
SAINT LOUIS 31, MISSOURI

Jan. 8, 1961

Dear Leon
and Velvet.

Thank you for your Christmas Card - it was so nice of you to think of us. We sort of lost contact and I didn't know where you were. Are you still globe-trotting or do you live in one spot?

Hope 1961 is good to you and your family. Wishing you the best of everything.

Sincerely

Phil Davis

Narda and sister Maja on right.

ESCAPES

Escape Gone Wrong

Leon Mandrake often performed escapes to promote his upcoming shows. During the early years, on a beach in Santa Cruz, California, his friend, Bernard Abrams, volunteered to escape from a straight-jacket while hanging ten feet off the sand. A crowd would gather, and ads for the Mandrake illusion show in the big tent nearby, would be handed out. Bernard was fond of all the bathing beauties on the beach and often gave impromptu swim instruction if interest were shown. As a result, he was frequently running late to start the escape, which was followed directly by the big tent show where he was required to assist. That day, he had come to the straight-jacket dripping wet. Before he could towel off, one of the assistants strapped him into it and hoisted him up. Because canvas shrinks when wet, the jacket grew tighter as he struggled. Every inhale made the cloth tighter about his chest. And, hanging upside down, the blood was running into his head. He screamed for help, but the beach crowd that had gathered assumed it was for dramatic effect and part of the show and they ignored him as they went off to the big tent. Luckily, Leon wondered why Bernard hadn't shown up and rescued his slowly rotating body from disaster.

Fortunate Escape

They had just pulled into town, Russel Point, Ohio. There was a performance scheduled that night in the nightclub, and there was just enough time to unpack, set up, and dress before opening at seven p.m. Leon parked the bus beside the club's back door. Everyone got out, including Velvet with Lonny, Ronny, and Kim, all under the age of three. Then on a whim, Leon said, "Let's grab a bite first before we start." Delighted at the rare change of routine, the whole group entered the restaurant across the street and started ordering off the menu.

Five minutes later, the whole back of the nightclub exploded and burst into the street. A rival club had just ruined its competition. The bomb would, undoubtedly, have killed many of the troupe had they set up right away as usual. As they gathered with the firemen and police to inspect the damage, they saw every window in the bus had been blown out. There was glass everywhere when they cleaned up and covered the window openings with plywood. After a few days, the Mandrake show moved on.

The Underwater Escape

It was in Clearwater, Florida, U.S.A. as Velvet remembers, about 1949. Leon was to be doing an escape from a trunk submerged in the hotel pool with news reel cameras catching the action.

Handsome as ever in his swimming suit, he was handcuffed and then bound with sixty feet of rope. The cameras were rolling. Down into the trunk he went and the lid was closed. Padlocks clamped shut. Then a rope around the trunk enabled the crane to slowly swing it over the pool. Foot by foot, it lowered the trunk until it hit the water and began to sink.

Velvet, pregnant with Ron at the time, was nervous when the seconds began to tick away. And then the water closed over the top of the sinking trunk. One minute......two minutes...... three minutes.....too long!

Leon recalled that the handcuffs were off in a second, but as the water started seeping into the trunk and he began working with the ropes, something went wrong. The rope began to float. Used to doing dry escapes on stage, he hadn't counted on that. It made it much more difficult to work. He kept getting entangled in the cord. In a sweat and finally a panic, Leon didn't remember what he did. His mind was a blank. Trying to take a last gulp of air as the trunk filled around his face, he got a mouthful of water. The trunk hit the bottom of the pool.

Velvet was about to scream for help, when suddenly Mandrake came swimming to the surface. He'd made it! The crowd went wild! Velvet helped him up the side of the pool nearly fainting with relief. As they took their bows, Leon whispered, "I'll never do that again!"

The camera man came over to shake his hand. "Well done, Mandrake! But the angles weren't great, can we do it again?"

"Absolutely not!"

The Rescue

In Calgary, Alberta, Canada, a young girl had joined the show as an assistant and had worked well with the rest of the troupe. But one night, someone saw her leave with a boyfriend and she didn't show up for several weeks. Concerned for her safety, they searched for her and asked questions about her in town, to no avail. After two weeks, the show had no choice but to move on in order to finish the tour.

A year later in Seattle, Washington, U.S.A. the Mandrake show had rented a large hotel suite, big enough for the whole group to grab some sleep after late shows. They had just finished two weeks in Olympia, Washington, had driven all night, set up in Seattle, and also did opening night there. At eight in the morning with everyone sound asleep in the rented suite, the missing girl knocked at their door. Narda, sometimes an early riser, managed to get up and answer. The girl said she had seen their ad, saw they were in town, and wanted to explain what had happened to her and to apologize for leaving so abruptly. As they were talking, they suddenly smelled smoke, and, within seconds, flames were shooting up through the floor vents. The room below was engulfed in fire. They shook everyone awake and through the smoky hallway, they scrambled down the back stairs. When they gathered on the sidewalk and decided to go to the cafe across the street, Narda realized she was barefoot. A soldier offered her his boots. (He picked them up later.) Everyone got out unharmed, thanks to the girl coming to knock on the door that morning. Had some strange power or twist of fate saved them all? She quickly disappeared after that and they never saw her again.

The Accident

"Somewhere in the mid states, we were driving through another small town," Lon recalls. "My brothers and I were probably playing board games on the floor of our large Packard limousine as we drove. This was well before the age of seatbelts. I can still remember the impact of the accident. Another car had run the light and rammed into us at an intersection. Its driver got out and walked toward us as Dad grabbed a notepad and pen and after checking that we were all right, got out to meet him. Even at six years old, from the back window I could see the man had trouble walking and when he got close, I could smell the alcohol on his breath.

"Before long, the man was pleading with my dad, 'Oh, please, please don't report thiss...I'm a very well-known lawyer in this town. No damage to your car, you shaid.'

"My dad was a good-hearted man and had a lot of empathy for others. 'We're all fine, no one hurt and these Packards are built like a tank – no damage.'

"'We'll forget the whole thing then, I'm so sorry,' the whining man kept saying. I wish now that I had gotten out and kicked him in the shin.

"We drove away watching the staggering man looking at his dented front end.

"About a year later, we were driving through the same town to repeat engagements farther on. Suddenly, a police car pulled Dad over. Expecting the usual small town speed trap, we were shocked when the policeman said he had a warrant for Dad's arrest. That sleazy lawyer had explained away his dented vehicle by saying he was a victim of a hit and run. Dad's license plate and description of our car had been given to the police and a warrant written for hit and run.

"Because I was so young, I didn't really understand how my dad convinced the policeman HE was actually the victim of a drunk driver. Using logic today, I suppose it was because he had written down the lawyer's name, address, and license number before the verbal agreement was struck. Even after a year, the paper was found in our glove compartment, which no one ever cleared out. A hit and run driver wouldn't have this information. Perhaps this, and maybe the lawyer's history of drinking and shifty ways, is what convinced the officer to let us go on our way.

Street Escape

In the Deep South states, the Mandrakes found a lot of people were rather superstitious and even nervous of magic. When Leon was walking down a sidewalk, he noticed a woman quickly crossing over to the other side of the street, saying, "Don't put no hex on me, no sir!"

Boxes and Tubes and Jails, Oh My!

One hot day in Miami, Florida. As a show promotion, Leon would be tied or handcuffed and placed in a wooden box or metallic tube to be nailed or sealed in. His record escape time had to be within three minutes. In the deep southern states he offered to escape from secure inner city jail cells. He would laugh as he remembered how the chief of police would search him for picks on entry and even stoop to secretly changing the locks at the last minute. Nevertheless, Mandrake escaped quickly every time.

The Idle Hour Escape

"In 1956, we were based in Alaska for a tour of engagements. We were there quite a while; Lonny went to school [grade one] in Fairbanks. I can still remember the shock we felt when we stepped off the plane into minus-forty degree temperatures.

"Back to Portland, Oregon and then Chicago for engagements, we then left the boys with my mother in Chicago and returned to Alaska with baby Geelia, just a year old, for a second extended tour. We were at the Idle Hour, a beautiful nightclub right in Anchorage. We were at the club setting up equipment, when suddenly a fireball appeared. A sheet of flames blazed across the middle of the club. Leon was on one side and I was on the other. When I tried to get to him, a woman, the owner, grabbed me and pulled me through the front door. I didn't know what had happened to Leon and was frantic until we saw that they had smashed a chair through a back window to escape. When I found Leon, his eyebrows were burned off, his hair was all singed, and his mustache was not what it used to be. When the ambulance came, Leon was rushed to hospital wrapped like a mummy (only his eyes could be seen). Later we realized that his face wasn't badly burned; it was just a little red.

"We lost our whole show. I had seventeen costumes accumulated over a long time. They went with the different acts and effects we worked on. All our props were gone. Many of them were of special value, because they were originals assembled by special craftsmen. They just couldn't be recreated in a short time. Searching the debris, we only found Leon's large magic rings of Canadian steel, charred but all right, and my exotic, silver, snake-shaped arm cuff Leon had given me. The Anchorage magicians' club felt badly for our loss, and they got together and donated enough props and illusions that we could continue performing."

REAL ESP?

In Chicago

Velvet remembers:

"We phoned Mama in Chicago right away to let her know we were all right in case she heard about the Idle Hour club fire in the news. She was so relieved, especially since our eight-year-old son, Lonny, had awoken crying in the night that he had seen a big fire and Daddy had run into the flames to save Mummy. He had been truly upset and frightened for his parents. We explained that Leon had gone into the flames to rescue one of the waitresses calling for help, a petite brunette who looked a lot like me."

At UBC

Lon remembers the Analytical Geometry class he took at UBC. The regular professor had broken a leg in Switzerland and his assistant had tried to take over with disastrous results. No one in the class could understand his accent, and many were having trouble with the course. "All 150 of us were dreading the midterm exam," says Lon. "Trying to study for it, I decided to study only the examples of each type of problem in the text. That would have to do. In the end, nearly everyone failed the test. I got a hundred percent and a scholarship. How did I know that the whole test would be made up of the text examples? It just came to me to study that. I don't think real ESP can be controlled, unfortunately."

(Lon did have some innate mathematical ability; earlier he had the highest mark in the province on the grade 12 provincial math exam.)

At the Magic Castle

Lon and I were performing at Los Angeles' fabled Magic Castle in 1995 and again in 1997, three shows a day for a week each time. . We were identifying objects in the audience, with Lon on stage blindfolded. Usually, I would ask someone if they had an interesting object and they handed it to me. I held it up for the rest of the audience to see, and then we waited to see if Lon could identify it or describe it in some way.

This time, the man flashed a coin in his hand then closed his fist tight over it. I thought *coin* and Lon picked up my thought and said it was a coin. But then I drew a mental blank; no information about it at all. I couldn't help Lon.

Suddenly, he began expounding on the coin – how old it was; yes, very old; dated in the 1600's; yes; found in a Spanish monastery while on vacation; yes; very valuable;...how did you know? ...The man and the rest of the audience were truly amazed, but no more than I.

After the show I said, "Wow, what happened out there with that coin?"

Lon said, "I don't know. It just sort of came to me."

We just stared at each other for the longest time.

The Magic Castle

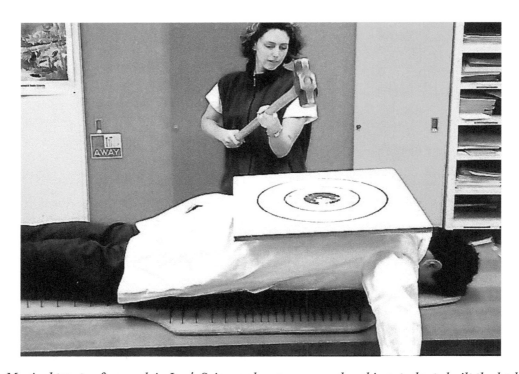

Magical treats after work in Lon's Science classroom; woodworking students built the bed of nails as required by Lon and then unexpectedly sharpened each nail to please? their favorite teacher. Here Lon relaxes on the very sharp nails as another teacher is asked to wack him with a sledgehammer. He was unharmed as usual.

After one of our shows at the Magic Castle with Velvet's cousin, Dolores Kreuger, Scottie Grace (Lon's grandmother's husband), Lon (standing) and Linda Mandrake. Below is the front entrance billboard at the Castle.

PEOPLE

The Mandrakes received an amazing number of Christmas cards and letters each year. They had met dozens of other acts over the years and many had kept in touch and some had become lifelong friends. Quite a number came to visit at Grosvenor Road; names like George Carl (world-class comic acrobat), Reveen the Impossibilist (hypnotist), the Zimmermans (magicians), Chang (magician), and Stan Kramien (magician and originator of the Magical Jamboree in Oregon). Nearly all provided happy memories; only a few were memorable for other reasons.

Impressions of Mandrake

Bernard (friend): "Leon was a socialist. He'd give you the shirt off his back."

Ronald (son): "Dad would give a job to anyone who needed one."

Velvet (wife): "When I asked Leon how much money he made with the fortune-telling, he said, 'They needed it more than me.'"

Narda (ex-wife): "Leon Mandrake was a kind man, but he was a soft touch."

Left to right, Leon, Velvet as a blond, Bernard Abrams above her with his wife Margie at the far right.

Nausea

Velvet remembers:

"We often traveled with a troupe of girls and most of them were really nice. But there was one that gave us a lot of trouble. Leon always looked for the best in people, but this girl challenged his faith in human nature.

"We were in Miami, Florida in 1949, doing two shows a night at a big theatre. I was expecting our second child (Ronald). I am a small person, and I always stood very straight and held myself in so that I didn't show very much until I was about six months. I had figured out how to move about in some of the illusions so that I could still do the escapes without hurting my stomach. Finally, we had another girl take my place.

"Leon had heard complaints from the other girls about this pretty, Italian-looking brunette, but he'd passed it off as silly jealousy. It was rumored that she had a young-girl crush on Mandrake and she seemed delighted to be chosen as replacement first assistant.

"The incident of the dress should have been a warning. My dad had paid for a beautiful, black, sheath evening dress that I wore before the pregnancy; our new assistant had admired it. Of course, I was upset when it went missing. And I was even more so when her mother came for a visit. Innocently, she mentioned that her daughter wrote home often and even sent presents, like the black dress recently – pity it was so small that she couldn't wear it.

"Then the girl had befriended a couple of shysters, who we believe had talked her into trying to sue Mandrake. A lien was placed on the show so that we could not perform or even leave town for our next theatre engagement. She was claiming that she had not been paid as first-assistant for months. They wanted a large sum of money to release the show and to allow Leon to continue his pre-booked theatre circuit.

"One day, the landlady of our hotel, who had been talking to her and didn't know the real story, accused me of treating the poor young girl badly. I felt so hurt and embarrassed. And I was so worried that these gangsters might try to hurt Leon. He was performing late at night, in a nightclub, while we waited for the court case to be heard. By then, I was nine months pregnant, looking after our one-year-old son, Lonny, and didn't need all this upset.

"In court, we surprised her by producing receipts signed by all the cast members that showed everyone including herself had been paid in full. Our good friend and show manager, Bernie Abrams, wasn't always so organized but, thank Heavens, he was this time. The judge scolded her for lying in court and trying to hold up the show, however, because Leon said that he wouldn't press charges, she was free to go. From then on we always referred to her as 'Nausea.'

"I went into labor shortly after that. Ronald was born on April 28th, 1949.

"Before we left the hotel for the road, the landlady apologized to me for thinking my husband and I had wronged the girl. She said the girl had really pulled the wool over her eyes, had seemed so charming, and then had tried to ruin her employer. And she then added, 'That girl even stiffed me for her rent.'

"Sixty-three years later we got a very surprising phone call from Nausea's daughter, who was planning, after her mother's passing, to publish a book of her mother's adventures. She was curious about the past, since some of the stories seemed inconsistent and she wondered if they were all true.

Nausea had claimed to be a big star in show business, been known as Narda, performed even in Cuba, and of course was married to Mandrake. We told the daughter that her mother had been Mandrake's assistant for a short time, that there was a real Narda, ex-wife of Leon, still living, and a current wife, Velvet, and that Mandrake had certainly never married her. The daughter said that her mother was prone to exaggeration and her list of marriages didn't seem to add up chronologically."

The Choreographer

A choreographer they had worked with visited the Mandrakes one year. He had come to New Westminster initially to be treated at the Hollywood l sanitarium He said he hoped Leon could help him with his paranoia. He stayed with them three months, never offering to pay for food, or a room, and running up huge phone bills to Los Angeles, Mexico, and Cuba. Leon finally asked him to help out about the place to earn his keep. The next day they wondered what he was up to; he'd spent the whole day in the garage painting a line down the middle of the two-car garage. Eventually, Velvet told Leon they could not manage with four children to support, and so the visitor was asked to return home. Mandrake handed him a paid bus ticket to Los Angeles. The day of the departure Leon also slipped him some cash for food on the journey. The reaction? The chap said, "Does that ease your conscience any?" as he pocketed the money, turned and boarded the bus. Lon, then seventeen years old, remembers how furious he was to see such ingratitude.

Note: The Hollywood sanitarium at 525 6th Street, New Westminster, operated from 1919 to 1975 and offered treatment for alcoholism and other addictions, homosexuality and mental conditions like depression. It was frequented by prominent wealthy members of society and even celebrities like singer, Andy Williams, actor Cary Grant, and the wife of senator Robert Kennedy, Ethel. It was one of the few hospitals to experiment with LSD.(source Wikipedia)

The Handyman

On another occasion, a chap who claimed to be a bit of a handyman, was hired to replace the drain pipes for the downstairs bathroom.

When he finished the job and then insisted the area be cemented over, several of Mandrake's friends began to wonder why the cement was necessary. Upon investigation with a shovel, Mandrake found that the chap had used inexpensive drain tile instead of proper plumbers' pipe; it would have leaked sewage and reeked for years. If the cement had been used as a cover up, it would have had to be drilled out to replace the faulty tiles.

Reveen, the Impossibilist

Peter Reveen came to British Columbia, Canada in the 1960s from Australia. He brought his wife and three children with him and planned to work as a stage hypnotist. He introduced himself to Mandrake and asked his advice on Canadian audiences and hypnotism in general. The two hit it off, and they became lifelong friends. The Reveen family even stayed with the Mandrakes before they got settled in. Reveen's career was a huge success, and he performed for decades in Canada and the United States as the "Impossibilist." As well as the stage hypnosis, Reveen showcased amazing feats of memory. On one visit to Vancouver, he told us he was studying French at night at the Berlitz School of Languages so that he could perform his entire two-hour show completely in French for his upcoming tour of Quebec. Reveen played all over B.C. and performed very many times at the Queen Elizabeth Theatre to a faithful return following, all hoping to be hypnotized by the master.

One summer, when Leon was quite ill with emphysema and in a wheelchair, he still made it to Reveen's show at the Burnaby Arts Theatre. After the show, Reveen greeted Leon with a warm, "It's good to see you, old friend," and they had a nice chat. It was Reveen who held a gala party in the penthouse of the Bayshore Inn and suggested to Bill Larsen that Leon

Mandrake should be recognized for his lifelong work in magic.

Reveen was named IBM's (International Brotherhood of Magicians) Magician of the Year in 2009. He passed away in 2013 at the age of 77. His son, Tyrone, has taken over his father's show to great reviews.

Celeste Evans

Celeste Evans, a rare and beautiful female magician, was born in White Rock, B.C. Actually, her sister married the stepson of Leon's Uncle Billy, so the family always laughed and talked of shirt-tail relatives. Celeste's career included a lot of work in Chicago. The Mandrakes often got a phone call from her when she was in town. After one of her shows, Celeste admitted to Lon, "With your dad in the audience, I was so nervous, everything went wrong!"

Ray Roch

Ray Roch (pronounced "Rock") said that years ago he was performing in a mall in Burnaby, B.C. Just before he went on, he noticed Leon Mandrake in the crowd. Ray has an excellent Flim Flam Foolery (confidence man act) with professional sleight-of-hand work and great humor. Nevertheless, he greeted Mandrake, saying he'd really have to do a good job if he were watching or words to that effect. Leon said that unfortunately he couldn't stay and left. After the show, Mandrake came up to praise the performance; he'd been in the audience after all. He said he hadn't wanted to make Ray nervous...and it worked. When Ray shared this memory with me, he added, "See, that's the kind of man he was – really kind." (see also page 120)

Martin Nash

Martin Nash was a fine sleight-of-hand performer, billing himself as the Charming Cheat. He usually did gambling magic and occasionally worked as a resource person with the police. He was a regular performer at the prestigious Magic Castle in Hollywood, California for years, winning Close up Magician of the Year. He was indeed one of the best card men in the country.

As a young boy, Martin had watched all of Mandrake's shows at the PNE. Lon says his dad used to help the promising sixteen-year-old with the entrance fees since the fair lasted seventeen days and Martin didn't want to miss a show.

Lon worked as an agent for his dad and Martin Nash, as well as Chief Dan George (actor), Broadfoot (Canadian Airfarce comedian), Steve Gidora (musician), and Lon's younger brother, Ron Mandrake.

Shawn Farquhar

Shawn has been a friend of the Mandrake family for years, starting perhaps with his friendship with Ron Mandrake. We have watched Shawn grow into the World Champion of Magic (twice!). He has been a powerhouse of energy in our area (starting up the Carl Hemeon Chapter 95 of the Society of American Magicians (S.A.M.) and working as executive of the Vancouver Magic Circle as well as at the international level. He is past president of the International Brotherhood of Magicians. Shawn was the first person to fool Penn and Teller twice on their TV show *Fool Us*. His magic has appeared on TV shows like *X-Files*, *Highlander*, and *Ellen*, and also movies including *Spooky House* and *The Fly II*. Shawn works all over the world for corporate clients like IBM and Konica as well as many cruise lines like Disney Magic Cruises. When he has a rare break from his international performances, he attends local magic events and often organizes them (such as magic conventions to bring in international talent for our pleasure). He has helped with websites, is a magical historian, and is a mentor for local young magicians. When Mary Ungerleider's forty-five minute film, *Mandrake, a Magical Life* (2001), needed close-ups of a magician's hands, Shawn was chosen as the best in the business. The man who knows everything about magic and everybody in magic – it's Shawn Farquhar (see also page 120).

David Copperfield

For his private museum collection, David Copperfield, the internationally famous magician currently based in Las Vegas, purchased Leon Mandrake's crystal ball, which had been given to Leon by Alexander, the Man Who Knows. Lon and our youngest son, Eric, travelled to Las Vegas to deliver it, along with Alexander's scrapbooks. Afraid to put the precious item in the luggage, Lon had packed it in a carry-on bag where he could keep a careful eye on it during the flight. You should have seen the reaction of the local small-airlines agent when he checked the bag. "What on earth do we have here?"

Lon explained it was a crystal ball used in magical performances. The man examined it closely, peering into its depths. Lon said, "Isn't it a fine specimen? Absolutely clear."

Suddenly, the agent announced there might be something dangerous hidden inside the ball. *What on earth could that be*, Lon and Eric wondered. Finally the agent's supervisor came over and gave them the go-ahead to travel with the crystal in their regular luggage.

Once in Las Vegas, David Copperfield gave Lon and Eric first-class seats for his show and afterwards treated them to a tour of his famous and very private magic museum. Lon and Eric were truly delighted. And I was so sorry not to have been able to be there too.

Dave Price was the curator of the Museum of Magical History in Nashville, Tennessee, U.S.A.

He was impressed with Mandrake from an early age and so was delighted when Lon Mandrake donated his father's top hat and wand to the museum. Eventually the establishment closed and the Mandrake memorabilia was sold.

Dave Price/4102 Idaho Ave/Nashville, TN 37209/(615) 297-7418

Dear Lon: Feb 13, 1999

I read your recent letter in <u>Magic</u> and I am happy to write this response.

When I was a boy of ten the Leon Mandrake show reactivated Nashville's last old vaudeville house "The Princess Theater" for a week, closing with a midnight show on Christmas night 1948. I saw the show a number of times during that week and, although I never saw your father again, he remains to this day one of the great magicians of my childhood.

As I was writing this I happened to think of one of his best effects- the production of silks by snapping each one to reveal another tied corner-to-corner with the first. He did this many times and filled the stage with colorful silks; I even recall his music for this effect; it was "The Saber Dance." It was one of the best things I ever saw in magic.

Among the dozen or so items that I have selected to keep for my old age, regardless of what I do with the rest of the collection, is a window card of Mr Mandrake advertising the above date.

I hope you will get some pleasure from these memories of mine; I know I did!

Sincerely,

Dave Price

As you see this letter is several weeks old; I just now got a friend to find your address on the Net. Or at least I hope "L Mandrake" is you!!

James Dimmare is a world famous award-winning manipulator and illusionist with "the style of Astaire and the cool of Sinatra". His specialty is birds; he is one of the greatest dove magicians of our time. Yet he says he was a weak, skinny boy picked on by schoolmates. Then he found magic and his life changed for the better. In Mandrake's office we found this charming letter written by a very young James Dimmer.

James Dimmer
WONDERFUL WIZARDRY

Dear Mr. Mandrake,

I am sixteen years of age and I'm a big fan
of yours.I have been in magic for about four years and
I intend to make it my career.I was wondering if I could
have the pleasure of visiting you,as it would be a great
honour.And if its not to much trouble I would like an
autographed photo of yourself.I do hope you allow me to visit
as I will be looking forward to it.

#14,21668 LOUGHEED HWY.
MAPLE RIDGE ph:467-2584

James Dimmer
JAMES DIMMER

Theo Clafin

Theo Clafin (1928 – 1997) was taken on as an assistant by the Mandrakes in Dayton, Ohio about 1948. The blonde, good-looking boy was a magic enthusiast. His parents had said he was a problem child, getting into trouble, until the work on the Mandrake show had begun to change him for the better.

Unfortunately, one night Theo decided to make it on his own – the easy way, he must have thought. After hours, he stole into Mandrake's change room and dressed himself up in the magician's regalia (probably the black cape and top hat or maybe the red suit). He gathered up some impressive props and headed out to have his own promo photos taken. Apparently, he left the show to book himself as "Theo Mandrake, son of Mandrake the magician" when the Mandrake troupe moved west. Velvet said, "Leon was really disappointed in the boy. We heard a few years later that he was in Leavenworth prison [a federal penitentiary in Kansas] for impersonating an army officer. We were contacted because he had written Leon and I down as family contacts on his forms."

Theo "Mandrake" owned and operated a magic shop called Mandrake's Magic Shop in Toledo, Ohio and performed under the assumed name for the rest of his life.

Pool Boy

Leon and Narda were in Los Angeles performing at the Orpheum Theatre in the early 1940s. They found that, in Beverley Hills, it was more reasonable to rent a house than to pay hotel room-rates for a company of performers. And so they rented the beautiful mansion belonging to Lowell Thomas, the star of the popular TV show, *Wild Kingdom*. It was a lovely house and grounds. The bar and pool were often filled with cast and friends and neighbors and out-of-work actors or dancers, who were hoping to make connections and perhaps work on the show.

Leon, meanwhile, was in overalls backstage at the downtown theatre adjusting and setting up equipment and props. When he got home, the place was full of guests as usual. Narda greeted him with a smile and said, "The pool's backed up again; I think the leaves from that tree have plugged the drain. Can you have a look at it?"

So Leon is down on his knees in his overalls checking the drain poolside when one of the guests strikes up a conversation.

"Oh, I'm here all the time. I'm a great friend of Mandrake, you know; known him for years, we're really close."

I think Leon's sense of humor would probably have let the chap chatter on, ignorant of his audience's identity.

The Rough Looking Character

Leon noted a rough-looking character at the bar and wondered why the club bouncers hadn't escorted the poorly dressed man out. As the chap became more and more belligerent, Mandrake pointed him out to one of the waitresses. She said, "Oh, him, why, that's Howard Hughes, he owns the joint."

Lothar

Mandrake's assistant, Lothar, was with the show from 1941 to 1944. He was a tall, well-built African American who often performed the substitution trunk act with Mandrake. Volunteers from the audience were asked to come up and examine the trunk and then help Lothar to step into it. A large sack in the bottom of the trunk would be drawn up around him and tied shut. The trunk was then padlocked and securely roped. Next, a curtain was placed around the trunk. Mandrake stepped up onto the trunk behind the curtain, counting "one, two".and then Lothar would appear in Mandrake's place, saying "three". When the curtain was opened, the trunk unlocked, and the bag untied, out came Mandrake wearing a different colored suit! The two men had switched places in three seconds.

One night when the show troupe entered a hotel in Reno, Nevada, looking for rooms, the clerk refused to allow Lothar, due to his dark skin, to stay on the premises. Mandrake told the clerk that if one of his troupe was refused, the whole group would not say there and walked out in disgust at the racial prejudice.

In 1944 at the height of World War II, Lothar was drafted. When he got out of the army, he worked as a male nurse in San Francisco. Below is the only photo found of Lothar. He is standing beside two assistants in a camel costume which was a comedic part of the Mandrake show.

Glen Stevenson

Mandrake met Glen Stevenson, a concert pianist originally from Saskatchewan, while working in Edmonton. He was impressed with Glen's talent and soon he became Leon's musical director for shows from 1976 to Mandrake's last show in 1985. Glen is a versatile performer with a repertoire from ragtime to the classics. He has performed on cruise lines and in numerous international hotels and clubs. Glen is currently based in Vancouver, where he performs as a soloist as well as collaborating with recent graduates of the UBC opera program. For Mandrake, he accompanied the hour-and-a-half to two-hour shows with music like the fast moving "Saber Dance," "The Poet and the Peasant," and Strauss waltzes, as well as Leon's original songs like "Every Day is a Holiday." Mandrake's show theme was written by Leon himself, and performed by orchestras and Stevenson. Glen, a long-time friend of the Mandrake family, is truly the man who can play anything. An audiovisual sampler of his music (especially his French medley) is found at glenpiano.blogsot.ca or he can be contacted at glenfingers@yahoo.ca .

Left to right: Francis Martino, unnamed magician, Dick Zimmerman, Carl and Lottie Hemeon, Leon ad Velvet Mandrake, and an unnamed magician.

THINK OUTSIDE THE BOX

One of Mandrake's talents was his ability to "think outside the box," that is, to see things in a different light or from a different angle to solve a problem. His creativity and easy escapes are evidence of this. When the family got together at our house for a holiday brunch, being an English teacher, I had devised intricate word games and puzzles. Leon always won the prize; he had a real talent for it – then, of course, he was an avid reader and had the ability to think outside the box.

The Medicine Show Character

Leon sometimes tried reinventing himself as a totally different character than a sophisticated magician. One year he became Doctor M. A. Duckcall, dressed in striped pants and a cutaway coat, with a goatee and horn-rimmed glasses. This fast-talking faker was a purveyor of Duckcall Tonic (an elixir that cured everything if you believed him). This was Mandrake's humorous look at a vintage bunko artist.

The Composer

Few people knew that Leon Mandrake wrote quite a few songs for the show; lyrics and music. His best, "The Mandrake Theme," had a big-band feel with a haunting melody.

The Writer

There are many pages of lecture notes and philosophies beautifully typed on a script typewriter by Leon. He was so fast and accurate, he carried the portable machine with him for making up contracts on the spot. For fun one summer, he and an artist friend, Greg Williams, collaborated on a comic book with a medicine-show theme and cartoon animals for leading characters.

The Lecturer

The best-loved Mandrake, other than the magician, of course, was the lecturer Mandrake. His university lecture series throughout the 1970s was amazingly popular.

THE LECTURE SERIES

Mandrake's university lecture series was amazingly popular with students wanting to know more about topics like the occult, gambling, false psychics, witchcraft, tarot-card readings, séances, fortune telling, confidence games, and dream interpretation. Leon had strong feelings about charlatans and religious zealots who preyed on the vulnerable. He vowed that the only power witchcraft had was the fear of it in the mind of the victim. At one point, he offered $5000.00 to be given to anyone who could demonstrate any action or happening that he could not duplicate or explain by natural means.

At the lecture series at Totem Park Residence at the University of British Columbia a female student asked a question, "How could a person shatter a rose other than with real magic?" She was apparently nervous of a self-proclaimed witch at a cult gathering, who attempted to prove her powers by shattering a rose with her mind. Leon asked her if it would alleviate her fears if he could shatter a flower right in front of their audience, using a magician's methods. She said it would make the witch's abilities less frightening.

Mandrake brought her up on stage and asked her to select a rose from the bouquet of roses decorating the stage. He waved his hand over the flower and its petals flew off in all directions. To those in the know, he was using Rupert's Pearls[1]; he did not disclose this, but said he was not using supernatural powers. The girl was noticeably relieved and was much less vulnerable to the likes of cult leaders and witchcraft.

Mandrake Quotes

"Always count your change."

"The smarter you think you are, the more vulnerable you are."

"You cannot cheat an honest man."

"The only game worth playing is strip poker – the more you lose, the more you have to show for it."

"Conscientious people can be found in any walk of life and stand out as a thing of beauty, like a butterfly in an outdoor toilet."

---

1   Rupert's Pearls: Rupert's Pearls are toughened glass beads created by dripping molten glass into cold water which makes it solidify into a tadpole-shaped droplet with a long, thin tail. If the tail is broken, the pearl explodes. Place one pearl in a flower, snap the glass tail and the flower explodes.

The Lecture Circuit

Many letters were written by the universities praising Mandrake's performances, most of them unsolicited. The following letters speak for themselves and give us an idea of the content of the lectures and the audiences' reaction.

UNIVERSITY OF WINNIPEG STUDENTS' ASSOCIATION

ROOM 230, LOCKHART HALL
515 PORTAGE AVENUE
WINNIPEG 2, MANITOBA, CANADA
TELEPHONE - 786-7537

November 5, 1970

Mr. Al Franklin
14106 Grosvenor Road
North Surrey, B. C.

Dear Mr. Franklin:

In responce to your letter of October 29, I would like to
say that we were very happy with Mr. Mandrake's visit.

The theatre was filled to capacity at both the lecture and
the show. On both occassions the audience responded enthusiastically. In fact, he was given a standing ovation
at the show; a very rare occurence at our university. His
demonstrations of extra sensory perception were outstanding
and led to much debate among the students after he left.
The entire event was beyond our expectations. Pass on word
of our appreciation to the Mandrakes.

One small business matter remains. Mr. Mandrake forgot
his book here, which we sent him with the understanding that
this cost would be met by you. The mailing cost was $2.26.
The Student Office awaits your reply.

Thank you again for arranging the visit. Send my regards
to the Mandrakes.

Yours truly,

Esther Nikkel

(Miss) Esther Nikkel
Director, Academic Affairs
University of Winnipeg
Students' Association

EN/do

WESTERN WASHINGTON STATE COLLEGE

August 7, 1973

Al Franklin
14106 Grosvenor
Surrey, British Columbia
Canada

Dear Al:

Just a note to again express our delight and satisfaction with Mandrake's appearance here this past year. His ability to communicate with people of all ages and backgrounds made his visit one of the bright spots in our program. I sincerely hope we can make room for Mandrake on our program in the future.

Sincerely,

Barry Bonifas
Program Coordinator

BB:as

The Students' Union
Memorial University
of
Newfoundland
St. John's
Newfoundland

March 14, 1978

Mr. Al Franklin
Tour Manager
University Artists
P.O.Box 516
New Westminister, British Columbia
V3L 4Y8

Dear Mr.Franklin:

It is difficult to express our appreciation at Mr. Mandrake's recent appearance here at Memorial.

He gave a talk that enthralled our medical, nursing and psychology students, and his evening performance to a general audience received a standing ovation (they are so rare that I hardly need say more). His warmth and humanity shine while he enthralls one with his artistry and sleight of hand.

Please call when another tour is planned that will come near our island — it would be very convenient if it were next February but we would not want to miss him anytime.

Yours very truly,

Ian Feltham
Entertainment Director
Council of the Students' Union

IF/ch

FRASER VALLEY COLLEGE

1979 11 26

University Artists,
P.O. Box 516,
New Westminster, B.C.
V3L 4Y8

Dear Al:

Thank you for introducing the members of Fraser Valley College
to the powers and wonder of Mandrake. These two noon hour
concerts were by far our most successful to date.

Many students, faculty and staff have commented on the quality
and polish of Mandrake's performance. Personally I was totally
enthralled by the delusions and couldn't help believing that
perhaps there is such a thing as magic.

I can safely say that Fraser Valley College thoughly enjoyed
Leon Mandrakes performance.

Yours sincerely,

Lorna A. Collins,
College Activity Coordinator.

LAC:kmr

WEST CAMPUS
34194 Marshall Road,
Abbotsford, B.C. V2S 5E4
(604) 853-7441

EAST CAMPUS
45600 Airport Road,
Chilliwack, B.C. V2P 6T4
(604) 792-0025

AGASSIZ CENTRE
7169 Cheam Avenue
Agassiz, B.C. VOM 1AO
(604) 796-2254

HOPE CENTRE
895 Third Avenue,
Hope, B.C. VOX 1LO
(604) 869-9991

MISSION CENTRE
33070 Fifth Avenue,
Mission, B.C. V2V 1V6
(604) 826-9544

Telex number for all campuses and centres is 04-363530.

The University of Manitoba Students' Union

University Centre
Winnipeg Canada
R3T-2N2
Phone 474-8330

Leon Mandrake
307 Carnarvon
North Westminster
B.C.

Dear Leon,

    Thank you so much for your wonderful performance here
last Friday (September 20th). I, and Wendy too, will treasure both
your Campo performance and the dinner we had with you and your wonderful
wife.

    3,000 people were really pleased at the opportunity to see you,
and reactions have all been very, very ecstatic! Thanx to you, our Campo
First Week program was an unqualified success...

    We're all really looking forward to seeing you again in
February. Maybe we'll pick you up at the airport in style this time.
('56 Chevys aren't too classy, are they?) Ah well......

    Please thank Al Franklin for me. He's undoubtedly the nicest
"manager" I've ever dealt with.

    Thanx again to you for bringing a breath of light and love
to our University. Anytime you feel like a chat, please feel free to
call me collect anytime...

                            Remembering,

                            BoB Harrison
                            Programming Commissioner
          The University of Manitoba Students' Union
                     (204) 474-8357

AND NOW.......

Narda Now

Narda has lived many years in Mexico. Still very active, she has several properties she rents out to others. At age ninety-six, she phoned us from her home over-looking Chapala Lake in view of the volcano Colima:

"It was this spring, just after I injured my knee. I had been in hospital for a while and was so glad to be back home to get a good night's sleep. Then something in the middle of the night woke me up. I realized there was someone in the living room. Three thieves had slid down a rope from the overhead skylight. Coming into the bedroom, they were surprised to find someone home. I'm a good shot, but

of course I was unarmed. One of them held a knife to my throat and said to be quiet or else, while the other two searched for electronics and valuables.

"After a while, I said to the young man, 'Why are you risking so much to steal a few hundred dollars of stuff?'

"'I'm poor. I'm hungry.'

"'Let me make you something to eat,' I said and went to the kitchen to make a sandwich for him. He ate it with thanks.

"After a while, the three left with my TV and stereo, but I was alive and well."

An evening out: Linda, Lon, Glen Stevenson, Velvet, and operatic performers Brandon Thornhill (bass-baritone) and Taylor Pardell (soprano)

THE REAL MANDRAKE THE MAGICIAN

Velvet Mandrake's Ninety-first Birthday

We were so pleased that Velvet, my mother-in-law, had settled into the retirement home and seemed happy there. She had made friends and, physically fit, was enjoying the walking excursions and yoga sessions as well as singalong music gatherings at the home. At ninety-one she was, and still is, a petite beauty with a quick sense of humor and ready laugh.

When her apartment had stood empty for a year, she and the family had all agreed to sell it. Because there were twenty-five years of memories in the place, we were hesitant to pack up her things for her and put them in storage. The photographs of the show in exotic locations like Thailand, things like tiny, size-five sandals with Hawaiian white sand still clinging to them, and her costumes, some in red or blue velvet with headdresses, really slowed us down. I had been going through a cupboard near the kitchen, sorting things for donation and finding a few things I could use, like candles and placemats. I saw a cake decorating set similar to one I already had and a tube of fine pink cake sprinkles. In a hurry that day, I threw the tube in my pocket. After all, the next day I would be baking Velvet's ninety-first birthday cake.

We put two long tables together to accommodate the fourteen family guests and decorated with streamers and fresh flowers. Velvet's favorite color, purple, was the theme.

She was delighted with the afternoon, surrounded by her children, three of her grandchildren, and four of her great-grandchildren. Eight-year-old Logan and her sister Rayne, six, were especially full of hugs for their great-grandmother, "Little Grammy." When I brought out the lemon birthday cake, aglow with candles, we all sang "Happy Birthday." I cut the cake, served Velvet, then passed a slice to my daughter across the table.

Suddenly Katrina said, "Wait!! No one eat their cake!"

We all looked up.

"Those aren't cake sprinkles, Mum! Did you get them from Grammy's apartment?"

She was clearing her mouth with a napkin. We glanced to make sure Velvet hadn't touched her slice.

"What?!" I exclaimed. We examined the fine pink crystals on the cake; up close you could see a miniscule pin hole in each tiny bit. They were show costume beads, the finest anyone of us except Velvet had ever seen. Luckily, the odd crunch with the first bite had warned us all. The icing was thick enough that we could clear off the top that held the "sprinkles" and still have the lemon cake with ice cream. However, even though I've made a hundred birthday cakes, I'll never live that one down! I've stopped using cake sprinkles altogether. I can still hear Velvet laughing.

307 Carnarvon Street

The home purchased by Leon Mandrake's Aunt Mildred at 307 Carnarvon St. New Westminster, B.C., Canada, was a base for his family for nearly a hundred years.

Over time, Leon renovated the home extensively, doing a lot of the work himself (carpentry, wiring, and painting) with the help of friends and his sons. The old wood stoves were replaced with a modern furnace early on, walls were resurfaced, and new windows installed. A new foundation was required. On the road a lot, Leon rented the property or had family live in the Victorian house. Lon and I redecorated it when we first married and we lived there fifteen years.

In 1994, 307 was sold to the Heritage Society of New Westminster. The Victorian house on its right side, a mirror image of 307, was also purchased by the Society to form a large complex to be used as a temporary home for the homeless and hungry. They built a joining section between the two buildings making room for offices, large gathering rooms, thirty-five beds (fifteen for offenders and twenty for the homeless or risk of homelessness) and a commercial-size kitchen. The exterior was painted heritage lime-green and was given landscaped gardens. I believe Leon Mandrake, had he known, would have been pleased.

Because the house had been initially built for the daughter of the captain of the Royal Engineers, who lived in it for three or four years, it was named after her...the Mary Keary House.

Realizing Leon Mandrake had a connection to the place, the organizers asked Lon to speak about the Mandrake heritage at the gala opening and picnic held in August 2013. We were given a grand tour of the complex with its state-of-the-art exercise room, long mahogany-board office table, many bedrooms, and an office in what had been our bedroom. The heat was supplied by a very modern geo-thermal heat pump dug into the backyard where the cherry tree used to be.

When the Heritage Society set up a walk of memorial plaques in the park along the river, we were pleased there was one for Leon Mandrake, magician. He truly was a famous son of New Westminster.

THE REAL MANDRAKE THE MAGICIAN

Mandrake's Home Burns

On a bright morning in August 2016, we received a call from a friend, asking if we had seen the news. We hadn't.

The old homestead at 14106 Grosvenor Road, Surrey, B.C. had caught fire during the night. The house that had been built by Leon's Uncle Billy and been his store for years, the house where Leon had nursed his ill mother, Harriet, before she died, and where Leon and Velvet had brought up four children and several grandchildren, had burned pretty well to the ground. No one was hurt. The current owners got out of the house, with pets, before anyone was injured. Even though we had sold the house twenty-two years before, when Velvet, a widow, moved into an apartment for more security, we still felt an affinity for the property. It was the scene of many precious family memories. We drove over from Delta, a fifteen-minute distance, to be horrified at the missing roof, gouged walls, and blackened interior. It was hardly recognizable. All the renovations Leon Mandrake had spent months on when the family first moved to Surrey for a permanent base, in 1957, were gone. Luckily, most of the show and family memorabilia was safe in a storage locker and, of course, in our hearts.

Prestigious Performing Fellowship Award

Leon Mandrake, Velvet, and Lon, flew from Vancouver, B.C., Canada to Los Angeles, California, U.S.A. in August 1978. Leon was to be presented with the prestigious Performing Fellowship Award by the Academy of Magical Arts in Hollywood.

The location of the ceremony was the Variety Arts Theatre on Figueroa Street. The black-tie, star-studded celebration has all the glamour and suspense of the yearly Oscar awards for the motion picture industry. Masters of Ceremony over the years have been Cary Grant, Betty White, Edgar Bergen, and Toni Curtis.

The president of the Magic Castle, Bill Larsen, sat with the Mandrakes. Leon performed two of his favorites, the floating table and Katy King, for the guests. Then the MC, Mark Wilson (a famous children's magician with his own TV show), called upon Leon to shake his hand and present him with an engraved plaque for a lifetime of magical achievement.

The evening before, staying at the Roosevelt Hotel nearby, the Mandrakes had dined at the Magic Castle where they again toured the wonderful Victorian nightclub with its seance room, intimate bars, velvet-draped performing parlors, and exclusive underground vault of universal magic memorabilia. One wall even displayed a poster of Mandrake the magician!

Memorial Service at the Edison Theatre

Leon Mandrake died in the night of January 27th, 1993 at the Surrey Memorial Hospital. About a week later, a memorial service was held for the magician. The Edison Theatre (now called the Paramount) on Columbia Street in New Westminster was chosen as a fitting location, since it had been the site of Leon's first magic show.

Early on the morning of the service, it was discovered the furnace in the ancient theatre was not working, and in January near the river – it was especially cold. Some local magicians from the two magic clubs, SAM and the VMC (Vancouver Magic Circle), came out to help warm the place with space heaters, thaw the bathroom pipes, and arrange flowers and food.

Over eighty people attended in the small theatre. Many came from the United States. Several phoned in their condolences, including Mandrake's old and dear friend Reveen, the Impossibilist, who was on tour and unable to attend. Several people spoke to the group at an open mike, including Len Lauk (former head of CBC TV programming), Sean Farquhar (twice World Champion of Magic), former assistants George Patey and Bill Eliason, and Lon. We all showed our respect for one of the last of the masters of magic, in company now with Houdini, Thurston, Dante, Alexander, and Blackstone. He will be remembered.

Velvet confided later that Leon "would have loved this....the furnace not working;[in show business] something always goes wrong."

The Broken Wand Ceremony

In the IBM membership (International Brotherhood of Magicians), it is tradition to hold a broken wand ceremony for a magician who has passed on. One was held for Leon Mandrake at the Paramount Theatre. The magician's wand is snapped in two, symbolizing that he no longer has need of it. It is usually given to the family, much the same as a flag is given in military ceremonies.

Honor Roll

Along the Fraser River in New Westminster, B.C., a walk has been established with name plates honoring the amazing people who have touched the city. Leon first performed at the Edison theatre on Columbia St. at eleven years old and then in many venues in Vancouver and the rest of the province during his lifetime. Getting his start here, Leon Mandrake was truly a son of New Westminster.

Grand-daughter Katrina remembers:

"I saw several performances over the years, however, probably my most vivid memory of my grandparents' show was when I was around the age of four. At home, Papa would do the odd magic trick now and then for fun with the grandkids, but to see them on stage, I think maybe for the first time for me then, dressed up in their costumes, was amazing. I remember sitting in my stroller, watching the empty theatre fill with countless people. I had seen the rings, other magic tricks, and various props for the larger illusions before, as well as the costumes, etc. [see also page 67], but now that everything had come together in the show, I saw not only my grandparents, but also Mandrake the Magician and his assistant, Velvet, as others in the audience saw them. I was so very proud of them.

"I remember my parents wondering about how my younger brother, Lonny, a little over one year old then, might react to the gun shot illusion, too young to understand that it wasn't real. [See page 19] Thankfully, he had fallen asleep after the long day near the end of the show before that part. I remember how the entire audience went silent, you could hear a pin drop, as the tension hung in the air as Mandrake lined up for the shot, Velvet standing between him and the board. The nervous look on her face held the audience, then the shot, her body jerking with the impact. You felt the emotional concern of the audience gasping in horror, and then their relief realizing that she was alive, and finally their astonishment and amazement as they saw the ribbon had passed right through her. Seeing other shows of theirs when I was older, I noticed after every individual part of their show, packed full of countless amazing things one after another, the audience would swell with an emotional delight that you could almost feel, their applause and reactions truly an expression of how they felt. At the end, they were talking about the different parts, and of how much they enjoyed it. Mandrake made the audience feel like they were part of the show and not simply watching it. It seemed to me as if he were playing a game of *if you think that was amazing, wait until you see this one*, each part becoming more grand and amazing than the last, with the roar of applause growing louder and larger the more the show progressed.

"It was fun growing up as a kid, because it was as if my grandparents had secret identities, like superheroes in a comic or T.V. show, Grandma and Papa turning into the amazing Mandrake the Magician and Velvet come show time."

The Mentalist's Assistant, Linda

The magician's assistant: this title always makes me feel like Walt Disney's Mickey Mouse in the wonderful *Sorcerer's Apprentice,* where Mickey is following along in his oversized magical robes trying to keep pace with the powerful wizard. Having been a magician's assistant for thirty years, I realize this mental picture is not too far off the mark!

As magicians, we approach the circular tables. Faces of the party guests look up expectantly.

"Good evening. My name is Mandrake. We will be entertaining for your pleasure after dinner. We are mentalists; we perform magic of the mind. Would you like to see a small sample of what we do?"

They welcome us enthusiastically. My husband skillfully spreads a deck of cards before one man and asks him to choose a card, any card, while his co-workers and their wives look on. I'm not needed for the card tricks. All I have to do is smile, look amazed when the magic climaxes, and shift my feet now and again so my high heels don't pinch. We have been doing shows a long time, and I know what to expect.

The client invariably greets us warmly, and chats about magic and my husband's famous father. We are treated as honored guests, offered alcoholic drinks that we always decline before a show, and given the option of having the sumptuous buffet along with the other guests. We locate the stage or performance area, set up a few necessities, and, on cue, begin to work. And

we enjoy it. We genuinely laugh when unusual objects are offered for our blindfolded identification or humorous lines come bubbling up unexpectedly. The audience enjoy themselves and their party mood is catching. By the end of the evening, we aren't feeling tired. On the contrary, we are flying high with adrenalin and excitement. The compliments flow as guests shake our hands. We were amazing, so they tell us, and by the end of the evening we are beginning to believe it!

I remember when we first started our career. We were fine, if we started performing right away, but if we had to wait a long time to go on, we got a little nervous. I would say, "You know, we could be sitting at home watching a good movie tonight and here we are!"

Lon would grin and say, "What the heck are we doing? I never dreamed I'd ever be doing this."

My main prerequisite for being a successful assistant to a mentalist was NOT to be noticed. This was the reverse of the flashy misdirection requirement for a regular magician's assistant. I usually wear a suit or subdued evening wear. If no one really notices me much, I have been successful.

Only on one occasion did a fellow acknowledge my involvement. And as might be expected, he was another mentalist at a mentalists' convention. He told me, "You look so innocent in your perky ponytail, but you can't fool me; you look like the girl next door, but I know...well done! Excellent job!" and he shook my hand.

The audience often speaks to me at the end of a show, especially if they are waiting to talk to the magician while he is surrounded with other patrons. I have often thought I should record all the different types of people that we meet.

There's the innocent. One young girl looked totally impressed with us and asked, "Are you two really psychopaths?" I grinned at her, in spite of myself, and, assuming she meant "psychic," I tried to answer her question.

And there's the not so innocent. I won't forget the man who was amazed at our apparent mental telepathy. "I think I know how you do it," he said and he jumped up suddenly and stuck his two fingers in my ears. I pulled my face back instinctively and felt he was being rather forward. When he said something about checking out my jacket and his hands were aiming at my waist, I stepped back and moved on to another table. I didn't think his wife looked too amused either.

And what if he had found something like electronics for example? Some mentalists rely on them. It could have ruined the illusion, indeed the whole entertainment for the evening. Occasionally, we find this strange competitive personality; they are out to prove they can't be fooled and that they are a match for the magician and want to do him one better. A wise and experienced entertainer knows how to handle this type; it is best not to set up a confrontational atmosphere to begin with. The personality of the mentalist is everything. If you let your charming self show through, the audience will like you and be with you. We've even experienced audience members trying to help us along saying, "No, really, you got it right, since I was thinking that first! Amazing!" Some people are intrigued and try to analyze what we appear to be doing (as at our performance for the Scientific Oceanographic Institute in Sydney, Victoria,

B.C. where we saw several scientists including some visiting Russian ones, taking notes and devising ways our apparent telepathy could be done). Others casually accept mental telepathy saying something like, "My aunt Mable reads tea leaves." Some have a belief system that cannot be altered; like a belief in supernatural powers or in their own abilities. Even some fortune tellers or readers come to believe in their own powers. At a mentalists' convention you see performers at different places along a graduated continuum. At one extreme end, they are giving their audiences the impression

they have real supernatural abilities, while at the other end performers begin each show with a disclaimer. Each mentalist has the problem of deciding where he stands. With Lon's scientific and teaching background as well as his father's magical heritage, he is an unusual species of scientific mystic. He can lecture with authority on the biology of the brain and yet he doesn't discount the possibility of mental telepathy.

Mentalism can draw the "kook fringe" as well. One evening at the end of a show a twenty-year-old girl came up to shake Lon's hand and tell him about her psychic experiences. She seemed agitated and we noticed needle marks on her arm. She spoke at length about jumping off the roof of the barn and confided to Lon, "I'm telepathic like you. I know you see them too; and you're afraid just like me." Then she saw the security man stepping closer and suddenly fled. He had been impressed with our show too and had come to meet us; when he saw her scurrying through the crowd, he said she was a regular, a bit of a kook. She had been terrified of him, mistaking him for one of the "others" coming to get her.

At another series of shows we were followed around by a most earnest and tenacious man who wanted us to give him winning lottery numbers. He assured us that he was honest and deserving. Lon finally threw him a humorous disclaimer: "If I could win the lottery at will, I'd be doing it." Still the man insisted. He was now convinced for some reason that Lon couldn't do it for his own personal gain. He followed us about for over an hour.

There are all sorts of employers as well. Most are charming, generous, cooperative, and organized. But we have had ones that do strange things like setting up the date and then not appearing, leaving arrangements at the last minute to uninformed assistants; one had suddenly gone on vacation; one had done no promised advertising at all; another, to our great surprise, had advertised us as hypnotists. One time, the promised stage did not exist. We arrived, expecting to perform two stage shows and instead ended up doing close-up magic to fifty individual tables. Many exhausting hours later, we realized that they had saved two plates of dinner for us, which we thankfully gobbled at midnight amid the chaos of kitchen cleanup. And the most important rule, when dealing with strange employers, is never assume anyone has a good microphone system.

Some regular magicians see mentalism as possibly an easier way to entertain because there is very little equipment to carry and set up. A deck of cards, some books, erasable boards, all fit into a briefcase. No heavy trunks, mis-matched lady boxes, and swords to lug about. But they also hear that the preliminary cooperative training for a double act is a lot of work and that often two-person mental acts split under the stress of the performance. Being highly critical and demanding of each other would be a death blow to the joint endeavor.

My husband and I are easier-going and more forgiving. We are flexible. The routine is not set to music and timed exactly as with a regular magic act. We adapt to the location, whether it's a theatre stage, a convention room, a rocking cruise boat, or a back patio, and we adapt to the audience. Thinking quickly on your feet like an improv entertainer or classic stand-up comic is a good comparison. Many a time the fast footwork necessary to cope with an unexpected challenge has been what made us laugh with pleasure at the end of the evening. We'd be saying, "When that happened, I couldn't believe it. Never ever happened before, but we did it! Did you see his face? That was incredible!"

And of course being able to camouflage a mistake is invaluable. We have once or twice seen an inexperienced entertainer draw attention to his error or failure and then apologize for his lack of practice of his magic! Horrors! This only serves to embarrass even the audience. Far better to cover with a substitution or a joke. With a little luck, the audience will think the disaster was deliberate and part of the show.

Unless magicians have studied it, they don't always fully understand mentalism. At magician dinners, I have had magicians casually ask me to give them the "secret" of our performance. They intimate they're in the know already, or that I owe them a response, or they say what they think we're doing, hoping I'll blurt out, "Oh no, it's not that, we're doing such and such." All I could think of at the time was that I wasn't very flattered with their obvious miscalculation of my intelligence. "Since brevity is the soul of wit" (to borrow Shakespeare's phrase), when they ask how we do it, I answer, "We do it very well." And then we can both laugh.

One night, during close-up work at a party table, I had been laughing at a set gag we have used for years. The customer told me later, he liked the show even more because the magician's assistant seemed to be enjoying herself so much.

THE REAL MANDRAKE THE MAGICIAN

Lon and Linda Mandrake perform at Science World

Winners of the Mandrake Trophy (1993 to 2018)

Shawn Farquhar: (1993, 1998, 2000, 2003, 2009, 2016) twice World Champion! (see page 91)

Julianna Chen: (1994, 1997) She emigrated from China in the late 1980s to live in Vancouver, B.C. When she attended a Vancouver Magic Circle meeting, several magicians told her she could be an assistant for them. She was a fit, attractive girl in her twenties. She politely thanked them but declined the offers saying, "I'll do my own show." Then she performed for them and "blew the members out of the water." She was China's magic champion and a former acrobat as well. When Lon invited Julianna to the SAM meeting at the Mandrakes' house, Linda noticed she was standing on her head in the dining room near the dish cupboard, explaining something to another magician, in complete control, strong and flexible. In China, she'd had an injury as an acrobat and so trained in magic instead. Her card manipulations (with cards spinning huge distances through the air) is world class. Lately, we only see her occasionally because she is an international star, winning first place in the international FISM[2] contest for stage magic, and performing in many areas including Las Vegas, France, Germany, parts of China including Hong Kong. Her televised changing masks routine always amazes us.

Rod Chow: (1999, 2006, 2017) He is well known in the insurance business (Jack Chow Insurance on Pender St. in Vancouver's Chinatown) in the thinnest commercial building in the world (six feet wide by a hundred feet long – *Guinness Book of Records* and *Ripley's Believe It or Not*). Rod, with his unique money magic, has won over forty awards, including first place in the SAM International Close Up Competition. Although busy with local shows, he continues to be our Assembly #95's faithful secretary.

Trevor and Lorena Watters: (2008, 2010, 2015) They have developed a delightful comedy act, which won them first place in the prestigious international contest for Siegfried and Roy's Golden Lion's Head Award. They work full-time as touring magical performers.

Ray Roch: (1995, 2012) He has performed at the Magic Castle and recently has published his autobiography, *Magic, Mayhem and Miracles,* featuring his new magic routine, "The Impossible Box." (see also page 90)

Lon and Linda Mandrake: (1996, 2007) Trained by Leon Mandrake as a rare and unique double mental act, Lon and Linda have performed in many venues in the Vancouver area, and as far afield as Science World in New York City. They performed twice in the Parlor of the prestigious Magic Castle in Hollywood, California. Lon, as president of SAM Assembly #95, has established the SAM Magic Club Performances at Science World for over thirty years as well as various magical charity performances in hospitals and for fundraisers.

Trophy Winners: Gary Savard (2001), Murray Sawchuck (2002), David Wilson (2004), Ray & Joanne Medway(2005), Henry Tom (2011), Chris Yuill (2013), and Jeff Christensen (2015).

---

2   FISM-Fédération Internationale des Sociétés Magiques

Lon with the Mandrake award given annually for excellence in magical entertainment and creativity

There are several magic organizations:

S.A.M. the society of (North) American Magicians was established in 1902 in New York at Martinka's magic shop. Its groupings are called 'assemblies' and many of these are in the U.S. although there are some in Canada and Japan. One of their early presidents was the famous escape artist and magician, Harry Houdini. SAM's monthly publication is MUM (Standing for Magic, Unity, and Might).

The I.B.M. (International Brotherhood of Magicians) was established in 1922 by Len Vintus (a magician from Winnipeg, Canada) with Gene Gordon (magician from Buffalo, N.Y.) and Don Rogers. It's groupings are called 'rings'. The international membership is about 13,000 to 15,000 magicians. The IBM's publication is The Linking Ring.

C.A.M. (the Canadian Association of Magicians) was established relatively recently by Joan Caesar in Toronto, Canada in 1997. Its membership and popularity are growing. It's publication is The Northern Peeks.

Many magicians in the greater Vancouver area (including the Fraser Valley), like Lon Mandrake, belong to all three organizations.

Society of American Magicians Assembly #95 named for Carl Hemeon: (2016-17)

Front Row:, left to right: Michael Glenister, Toni Chris, Ray Roch (Treasurer), Lon Mandrake (President), Ice MacDonald (International President of S.A.M.), Shawn Farquhar (twice World Champion), Rod Chow (Secretary), Rick Mearns.

Second Row: Jens Henrikson, John MacMillan, Anthony Young, Alex Seaman, Trevor Waters, Dave Waters, Kelvin Ng, Jeff Christensen, Billy Hsu, Juan Garcia, Denis Hewson, Glen LaBarre, Henry Tom. Missing: Jamie D. Grant, Paul Romhany, Ed Silva-White, and Chris Yuill.

Assembly #95 has performed at Science World in Vancouver, B. C. during Christmas and/or Spring Break vacations for thirty years. The popular magical attractions greatly increase the number of customers Often there are crowds lined up outside waiting to get in. Attendance can jump with the magicians to 5000 a day. They bring in extra staff to handle all the visitors.

MANDRAKE
The Great Mentalist
Real Magic Of The Mind

THE REAL MANDRAKE THE MAGICIAN

TIMELINE

1890s: John Wagner and Rebecca McDonald with her mother, Annie, and six children move from Nova Scotia to New Westminster, British Columbia, Canada

1901: John Wagner declared lost at sea

1905: Harriet Wagner marries Alfred Jackson

1906: San Francisco earthquake

1907: Carl Jackson is born

1911: By this time Harriet has divorced Jackson and married Arturo (Arthur) Giglio,Son, Leon, born April 11th on Whidbey Island, Washington

1916: Harriet divorces Giglio and returns to New Westminster

1919: Leon receives a magic set from his Aunty Mil for his eighth birthday

1920: Candy store owner, Stephen Linkert, helps Leon with magic

1922: Leon's first magic show at the Edison Theatre as Dewiz, age eleven

1925: Leon is the star magician at the PNE. age-fourteen as Dewiz, Leon or Jackson

1926: Houdini dies on Hallowe'en; Leon knew his wife, Beatrice

1927: Leon joins the Ralph Richards tour and then works his way home as a

magician on his own from Winnipeg, age-seventeen

1932: Leon's brother, Carl, dies mysteriously at age twenty-five

1933: Speak-easies; Leon's father dies of heart attack; Leon has car accident

1934: Comic, Mandrake the Magician, begins

1937: Leon visits Alexander, the Man Who Knows, in Los Angeles

1939: Mandrake serial films starring Warren Hull, Lothar actor is East Indian

(African Americans at this time not allowed in film)

1940: Leon marries Lola Narda Wilson in Seattle

1941: Darker-skinned assistant, Lothar, refused hotel lodging, Mandrake protests

1942: Leon performing in Reno; friend & manager, Bernard Abrams;

1943: Puppets lost in fire in Arizona

1944: Leon and Narda living in Hollywood; sells father's farm; visits Alexander; Lothar drafted

1945: MCA management (tour with Narda);

1946: Leon and Narda divorce; Leon hires Louise Salerno, former Blackstone assistant, in Chicago as replacement

1947: Leon and Louise (Velvet) marry in Kansas City; MCA tour with Velvet

1948: First son, Leon Jr., born in Chicago

1949: Second son, Ronald, born in Florida; first underwater escape, Florida;

performed in Texas

1951: Alexander's magic & name; third son, Kimball, born Ohio; Beniamino Gigli dies

1952: Mandrake movie starring Coe Norton as Mandrake

1953: Alexander dies

1954: Fire in Idle Hour club in Alaska; TV work as well as guest spots on children's shows

1955: Daughter, Geelia, born; Family meets Phil Davis, cartoonist; TV Alexander show

1956: Alaskan tour; Uncle Billy dies

1957: Hawaiian tour (six months),family moved to Uncle Billy's store Surrey, B.C.

1958: Assistants George Patey and Bill Eliason: creative illusion builders;

1960: Leon's mother, Harriet, dies of breast cancer at age seventy-two

1961: TV work: CBC; pilot; "Doorway to Nowhere" illusion on Mandrake show

1962: Seattle's World Fair; military bases west coast, Cal.; CBC pilot; Van. hotel

1963: TV special; PNE in Vancouver (ten years running); Harrison hotel and hot springs; the Cave night club in Vancouver

1965: Leon in hospital for bleeding ulcer in Toronto

1967: Aunty Mil dies at age eighty-nine

1967: Orient four-month tour (Japan, Philippines, Thailand (Siam), Indonesia etc.)

1969: TV show *The Manipulators*

1970: Son, Leon, graduates from UBC, Bachelor of Science; Mandrake university lecture circuit; TV show *The Manipulators*

1971: TV show *Mantrap*

1972: TV CBC Hallowe'en special

1974: Spokane World's Fair

1975: University lectures

1976: Leon's first grandchild, Kala, born to son Kimball and Jamie Ulrich

1977: Second grandchild, Katrina, born to Leon and Linda; TV *Beachcombers* episode

1978: Leon and Velvet receive Performing Fellowship Award for lifetime in magic

1979: Leon's cousin, Evelyn, dies; grandson, Sean (Ron and Cecelia Campbell); granddaughter, Jade, (Kimball and Jamie Ulrich) born

1980: Grandson, Leon 3rd (Lonny), (Leon and Linda) born

1983: Grandson Jerome, (Ron and Cecelia) born

1985: Chocolate Festival; TV Fifth Estate; Leon's last show; Leon diagnosed with Emphysema

1986: Expo '86 in Vancouver, B.C.

1987: Mandrake's first son, Leon, begins magic career (mentalist) at Science World

1988: Grandson, Eric, born (Leon and Linda)

1991: Old friend, Reveen, visits Leon and Velvet

1993: Leon, Mandrake the Magician, dies Jan. 27th at the age of eighty-one

1994: Aunty Mil's house (307 Carnarvon) in New Westminster sold

1998: Sheldon O'Connell's biography of Leon, *Mandrake the Incomparable*

1999: Great-granddaughter, Shyann, born (Katrina and Ian Coulas)

2001: Mary Ungerleider's film, *A Magical Life*; great-grandson, Ethan, born (Katrina and Stacy Johnston)

2005: Mandrake's son, Ron, dies of leukemia; eldest son, Lon, retires from teaching high school science.

2007: Great-granddaughter, Logan, born (Katrina and Jason Parleir)

2008: Velvet moves from Grosvenor Road to an apartment; home on Grosvenor Rd. sold;

2009: Great-granddaughter, Rayne, born (Katrina and Jason Parleir)

2013: Aunty Mil's house (307 Carnarvon St.) gala heritage house opening

2014: Great-granddaughter, Kalie, born (Sean and Crystal Loving); Velvet enters retirement home

2015: Velvet's apartment sold

2016: Grosvenor Road home (new owners) burns to the ground

2018: Great-granddaughter, Lia, born (Sean and Crystal Mandrake)

2018: Linda and Lon Mandrake write a biography of Mandrake and Velvet

1911   LEON MANDRAKE   1993
NEVER LOSE THE MAGIC IN YOUR LIFE
IN MEMORY – YOUR LOVING FAMILY

(photo courtesy Jerome Mandrake)

Linda Redden, originally from Chester, Nova Scotia, met Lon Mandrake, at UBC. They married, both had careers as high school teachers, and raised three children. As well, they have performed professionally as mentalists for over thirty years. Lon had fascinating stories of life on the road with his father, Mandrake the Magician, and family. Linda liked to write. So finally, they collaborated on this humorous and sometimes shocking look behind the scenes of the Real Mandrake the Magician.

9 781525 534706